Black and Female

by the same author

NERVOUS CONDITIONS
THE BOOK OF NOT
THIS MOURNABLE BODY

Black and Female
Tsitsi Dangarembga

faber

First published in 2022
by Faber & Faber Limited
Bloomsbury House
74–77 Great Russell Street
London WC1B 3DA

Typeset by Typo•glyphix, Burton-on-Trent, DE14 3HE
Printed and bound by CPI Group (UK) Ltd, Croydon, CRO 4YY

A CIP record for this book
is available from the British Library

ISBN 978–0–571–37319–2

MIX
Paper from
responsible sources
FSC® C171272

2 4 6 8 10 9 7 5 3 1

To my mother, Susan Ntombizethu Dangarembga
To my sister, Rudo Dangarembga
And to Sheri and Ines, whose journeys demanded
much that is unspeakable

Contents

Introduction
1

Writing While Black and Female
17

Black, Female and the Superwoman
Black Feminist
65

Decolonisation as Revolutionary Imagining
109

Notes
153

Acknowledgements
157

Introduction

I am an existential refugee. I have been in flight since I left the womb, and probably before, given the circumstances I was born into and the effect of these circumstances on my prenatal environment.

At the time I was born, my parents lived in Murewa District, an hour and a half west of Harare, where they both taught at Murewa High School. The high school was located at a mission established by an American Methodist Episcopal Church (AME) missionary in 1909. I was born in a hospital at Nyadire, another AME mission a hundred-odd miles from where my parents worked, located in the extreme north-east of the country. By the time I was born, the same church, whose headquarters were and continue to be in the United States of America, had merged with two other Methodist denominations to form the United Methodist Church (UMC). My parents were staunch members.

The country itself, Southern Rhodesia, was still a British colony then, albeit a self-governing one, a status that had been achieved in 1923. As a result, the colony had its own parliament, civil service and security services, which answered to the settler administration, and not to the British government, as previously had been the case. Today, opinions about the nature of British colonial policy at the time differ. Izuakor tells us how the official colonial policy of the European settlement of Kenya, adopted in 1902, resulted in an increase of the European population from approximately one dozen in 1901, to 9,651 in 1921, against roughly 2.5 million Africans, and that despite this preponderance of African people, a system of European paramountcy was entrenched.[1] Whaley, on the other hand, argues that the policy of supremacy of African interests was the guiding principle of all British colonisation on the continent, with Rhodesia being the exception.[2] Whaley's assertion relies on a white paper issued by the British Secretary of State for the Colonies, the Duke of Devonshire, whose purpose was to shift paramountcy in the British African colonies away from the colonialists to the African population, and on three key pieces of Rhodesian legislation,

4

which he refers to collectively as the Constitutional Documents, that entrenched separation of races. The white paper was issued in 1923, the same year that Southern Rhodesia was granted responsible government. According to the constitutional arrangements agreed upon between Britain and her colony that opened the way for this responsible government, Britain retained the right to intervene in the colony's legislative affairs, particularly in the case of 'native' affairs. In reality, however, it did not act to counter the white supremacist tendencies the colony soon exhibited.

Racist legislation enacted less than a decade after Southern Rhodesia became self-governing included the segregationist Land Apportionment Act of 1930. This Act divided the colony into 'European', 'Native', 'Undetermined', 'Forest' and 'Unassigned' areas. In addition to these divisions, the act prohibited Africans from purchasing land in European-designated areas. This might not have been punitive had the act provided for sufficient purchase land to meet the needs of the African population, which was not the case. Unjustifiably – except by the tenets of white supremacy – Africans in the country were afforded the right to purchase land without competition from the settlers in only 7 per cent of the country. This was to become an abiding grievance in the African population, and ultimately a primary cause of the Zimbabwean anti-colonial armed struggle that began in April 1966 with a battle in Chinhoyi, a small town roughly a hundred miles north-west of Harare. The conflict escalated into a bloody guerrilla war that raged on until a settlement between the nationalists and the Rhodesian government was reached at the Lancaster House Conference at the end of 1979.

After 1923, space and body continued to frame access to rights in Rhodesia, in spite of the British government's right to intervene. The country became a quasi-state with invisible internal boundaries that were consolidated into fact by legislation. The cities were generally seen as European territories. Africans, who resided in special African areas – the townships – came to be regarded very much as immigrants in these areas. Effectively, certain areas of the country were rendered both symbolically and legally white, a convergence that excluded the presence of unregulated black bodies in these areas. Conversely, the spaces where Africans were allowed some mobility – which included the reserves and locations on the outskirts of the urban areas – were ideologised as primitive, backward and under-developed, containing people who belonged to the category 'other'. The control necessary to keep these two realms of existence separate was exercised both officially and unofficially.

A pass system had been introduced to the country almost immediately after colonisers arrived in the area that is now Harare in 1890, while actual pass certificates were introduced in the 1930s. Rhodesians referred to these early colonisers as the Pioneer Column. This column was an army of some five hundred white men raised by Cecil Rhodes through his British South Africa Company (BSAC). Their purpose was to annexe the country they marched into for the British Crown. Cecil Rhodes himself was prime minister of the Cape Colony, in the south-west of what is today South Africa, from 1890 to 1896. Pass laws had been introduced into the Cape Colony in 1760 by the Governor Earl Macartney, an Anglo-Irish colonial administrator and diplomat, in order to control the movement of slaves in the colony, and were sub-sequently extended to prevent African people from entering the area. In introducing the pass laws to the newly annexed territory on arrival, Rhodes continued an entrenched British tradition of segregation.

Passes are tantamount to a kind of internal pass-port system. In the beginning, Rhodesian pass laws applied only to African men. The pass book that African men, and then women in urban areas, came to be obliged to carry stipulated where an African could work, where they could live and whom they could marry. My father was a man who, by the law of the land, was obliged to carry such a pass book in the country where he was a citizen. Control of physical mobility was a crucial tactic in Rhodesian white supremacist strategy. My mother told me of an incident in which, as a secondary school student in the 1940s, having returned to her family home in the Eastern Highlands for the holidays, she took a trip to nearby Umtali town, as it was then known, although it is now called Mutare. As she walked through the streets, a group of white youths struck her and pushed her from the pavement into the gutter.

Physical mobility and access to land were not the only areas of African life that the Rhodesian settler government controlled. Education was another such area. After the 1923 grant of responsible government, the colony turned away from the South African model of education that had been practised up until then, to prioritise high standards of secondary education, with a view to giving their children life opportunities similar to those enjoyed by British youth. On the other hand, government schools for Africans initially confined themselves to teaching agricultural and industrial skills. The first academic secondary school for African youth was opened at St Augustine's, an Anglican mission near Penhalonga in the Eastern Highlands. The year was 1892. The good results the pupils at the school obtained propelled the government to provide more secondary academic facilities for African pupils. Goromonzi High School, near Harare, was opened in 1946, while Fletcher High School, in Gweru, followed in 1957. My mother was one of the early students at Goromonzi High School. She was attacked by the white youths during one of her school holidays. Back at school after the shocking incident, when her class was asked to write an essay about the holidays, my mother narrated the episode with outrage and anger. Later she was called to the headmaster's office to be told that such stories were inappropriate and to be instructed never to write reports of such incidents again.

Institutions of education in Southern Rhodesia were segregated, as were many other institutions in the country. Desegregation initiatives were left to a group of white citizens, who endeavoured to introduce a system of gradual change that avoided the worst aspects of apartheid practised by the government in the neighbouring Union of South Africa. The ultimate goal of these citizens was to create some sort of multiracial society. The desegregationists were of the opinion that white rule had had a civilising effect on Africans, and that this new civilisation showed in African behaviours and institutions. In the words, written in 1960, of Edgar Whitehead, who was at the time both Prime Minister and Minister of Native Affairs of Southern Rhodesia, 'A new phase is now becoming apparent among the Africans, and that is in their institutions. This change is reflected in their ability to work together in organised groups, to cooperate, to be constitutional, to subordinate personal advantage to communal or civic ideals.'[3]

Whitehead's assertion points to the idea pervasive in Southern Rhodesia's white population, that besides these emergent, cultivated Africans, there existed in the country Africans of another sort. According to Alan Cousins, generally three kinds of African were perceived by whites: the 'civilised', the 'nationalists' and the 'masses': 'The "civilized" were said to be a very small group, just emerging, who did not support the nationalists.' A characteristic of these civilised Africans was said to be that they were moderate, alongside an assumption that their affective and cognitive dispositions corresponded with European values and sentiments. The nationalists were seen as unstable, criminally inclined, loud-mouthed extremists who wished to arrogate power to themselves. These fearsome nationalists were also said to be a small group, so that in settler ideology most of the African population fell into the undifferentiated, de-individualised category of 'the masses'. They were said to be a happy lot, contented with the progress made for them under colonialism, who cheerfully supported the settler government and harboured no interest in politics.

———

The introduction of British colonial rule in Africa coincided with the latter stages of the Victorian era. During this period there was a strong religious drive for high moral standards driven by nonconformist churches, including the Methodists and the Evangelical wing of the Church of England. Values included faith, charity, respect and a strong work ethic, which combined to construct a notion of an exemplary citizen plentifully endowed with dignity and self-restraint. In Southern Rhodesia these ideas of morality and decency were foisted on the African population for the benefit of the Rhodesian state. From a white settler point of view, African women were seen initially as victims of African men. These men were ideologised as beings who resorted to violence at the slightest provocation and who had little if any desire to work. This ideologisation of African men was necessary to justify the harsh control established over African men's bodies from 1890 onwards, and their coercion by various means into the labour that the capitalist colonial project required. Thus African women were at first seen as the prey of these men, who imposed heavy socio-economic demands on them, from which the women should be rescued. The system of migrant labour that African men were forced into, however, led to rising incidences of social challenges, such as sex work and venereal disease, prompting the white supremacist imagination to invoke in African women a 'natural immorality' to account for these phenomena, which its system of capitalist production had precipitated.

The BSAC adopted a policy of granting missionary organisations large tracts of land from the outset. It is likely that this was because the company recognised that Christianity, with its doctrine of meekness and turning the other cheek, would have the salutary effect of taming the land's African population, thus rendering the people more readily available to meet the company's need for an abundant supply of cheap labour. Indeed, these missions turned out to be locations that undermined the existing personhood of the African populations. In 1902, the Reverend J. W. Stanlake wrote that comprehending the notion of sin and the need for salvation could 'only be to the native mind a gradual awakening, hence conversational methods are likely to lead to more definite results than what is generally understood by preaching. Our work is similar to the submarine engineer; it is out of sight. We are undermining. Sometimes the unexpected happens. Our work is put back, and we must start again.'[4]

The mixture of colonialism and religion that gave rise to mission culture in Southern Rhodesia shaped my parents' trajectories, and the trajectories of the many other Africans who were influenced by mission life through their desire for education. The entire construct was, intentionally or not, fundamentally malignant. Little good has emanated from the foundations of colonial society as they were laid down in Zimbabwe. Today Zimbabweans struggle against those who took over the edifice of the colonial state at independence.

I was born, then, into a vicious society that constructed me as essentially lacking full humanity, needing but never able, as a result of being black-embodied, to attain the status of complete human. This is the environment I was raised in. It is these malignancies, their foundations and their effect on my life and the lives of other black-embodied human beings that I trace in these essays. In the first essay, I examine how writing has become for me a continual analysis of the interconnectedness of my personal and my national history. In the second essay, I describe how the trajectory of Zimbabwean society from the colonial to the post-colonial has impacted the position of women in both private and public spaces, and has constrained the competence of Zimbabwean women to develop, benefit from and celebrate their female as well as their human agency. In the third essay, I discuss how decolonisation is first and foremost a discursive event that must take place in the imaginary before society can expect to engage in the process of decolonisation in a manner that yields inclusive goods to the earth's human and other creatures, and to the earth itself.

I have been in flight from the malign realm of the imaginary that constructed, first, colonial Rhodesia, then the Republic of Rhodesia and their successor – militarised, elitist Zimbabwe – for as long as I have existed, wherever my body has been situated. I do not know the destination of my symbolic migration and doubt that there is one given the current construction of global society. The following essays are a location in the invisible geography of my asylum.

Writing While Black and Female

The first wound for all of us who are classified as 'black' is empire. This is a truth many of us – whether we are included in that category or not – prefer to avoid. Today, the wounding empire is that of the Western nations: the empire that covered more than 80 per cent of the globe at its zenith in the nineteenth century. It includes the British empire that colonised my country Zimbabwe in the 1890s. I was born into empire: my parents were products of empire, as were their parents before them, and their parents before that, my great-grandparents.

A major, early objective of empire was what it called 'trade'. Trade is premised on desire. Desire without love dwindles into lust, and empires, being impersonal, cannot love. Lust – impersonal desire that demands satisfaction – is dangerous at every level: the personal, the social, the global. Imperial lust has wounded every part of the world that empire touched, and today we know it has wounded the very planet that is our home. Thus has empire mutilated not only those it sought to subjugate, but also itself. This is the second wound that affects us all. We are yet to learn how to heal from the effects of an institution that stretches back into the time before we were born, but whose systems still work to disempower, dispirit and dismember. How this can be done is a question very few dare to ask because, quite apart from not knowing the answer, it often seems there is none.

Toni Morrison described certain horrors experienced by some of humankind as unspeakable, but today those subjugated by empire speak. This speaking exposes imperial systems and strategies whose purpose has long been to hide the effects of race in the world. While black people lead in that area of scholarship and activism, others, including white men, though they may kick and scream, are prodded to discuss the world's racialisation. Those who, like me, were wounded by the hubris of whiteness no longer say, 'I hurt,' and self-medicate in self-destructive ways, or act out a ruinous, enraged and bitter pain on our communities, as that hubris demanded. Today we say, 'You hurt me,' words that point not to the abjection and death that follow relentless self-mutilation, but to the possibility of removing oneself from the one who hurts, and thereafter transforming oneself into someone the one who hurts can no longer dismember.

'Look!' we who are black or brown are frequently admonished, now that that which was unspeakable is finally being spoken; 'Why do you speak of damage? Here are the roads, the hospitals. You can read and write; you have medicines. How can you speak of damage?'

Even before any black or brown person was assimilated into the academic systems of imperial education, and before spaces had evolved in empire where these questions could be asked, we had an answer. We said, 'We feel it.'

In Steve McQueen's 2013 biographical film *Twelve Years a Slave*, Patsey is an African-descent woman enslaved on a plantation owned by Edwin Epps. At her arrival she is in visible grief at being separated from her children. Mrs Epps orders Patsey be given something to eat to hasten her forgetting. Patsey's grief is an intense statement that screams, 'I feel it.'[1] To Mrs Epps, Patsey's grief is simply another instance of meaningless dysphoria amongst household creatures to be dealt with like onion peelings that have fallen to the floor, or dust that settles under the bed: it must be swept away. Patsey's statement of affect is ignored.

Empire could not bear to hear our screams because it knew it caused them. On the one hand, our expressions of pain are our proof of our living, proclaiming that we are hurting but still breathing. This is why there is a saying in Zimbabwe, *chikuru kufema* – 'the big thing is to breathe'. That which is dead does not feel. We are not dead while we protest. On the other hand, our expressions of pain are a direct threat to the systems of Western empire that rely on the illusion of giving, to obtain for itself the best that it covets in the domain of other people. Our expressions of pain say, 'This is not a gift.'

Healing is weaving, a knitting together and reintegration of the parts that were mangled and crippled. Weaving of words – and through this process, reweaving time, action and reaction into a new whole – makes writing back against empire a site of potential for healing. Some writing raises a scar, puffy, often suppurating, over the damage. The best writing opens the lesion again and again and cleanses. Here the trauma subsides with each set of words, sentences, paragraphs and pages. The rawness is transformed into something that in a certain light looks like skin that was never lacerated. What is done is done. Such transformation is our best option in this era.

The ravages of empire stretch further in time and space than we usually care to imagine. Tales of enslavement of African people by European slave traders are common, hurtful knowledge today. We have heard of the atrocities practised on black bodies that disembarked on the eastern coasts of the Americas. The history of the transatlantic slave trade is the history of empire, thus it is preserved and increasingly known. So central to empire was human-trafficking in black bodies that its officials kept meticulous records of the human beings it trafficked.

On the other hand, much less is known of the destruction this human-trafficking inflicted within the homes, communities and polities from which black bodies were coerced against their will into enslavement. Generations mangled by slavery exist on the Atlantic Ocean's east coast as well as on the shores of the Americas. The African continent lost large numbers of its population due to the transatlantic slave trade. The figure is estimated at 13 million of the continent's people. Imagine the whole of Sweden's population kidnapped. Or Greece's. Or Portugal's. Then add Slovenia or Latvia. The people ripped from their families for the purposes of unpaid labour in the Americas were amongst the strongest and most able-bodied individuals in their communities. They were people sturdy and healthy enough to stand a good chance of surviving a perilous journey to the slave ports on the African coast. Following that, they would need to withstand passage across the ocean in deplorable conditions, while retaining the capacity to work on arrival in the Americas. Brain drain, the emigration of significant numbers of numerate, literate people from a population to work in the globe's north-western quarter of the world took place in the last century and a half. During four centuries of transatlantic slave trade, bodies were drained from Africa. This drainage of the human population had disastrous effects on the continent's agrarian communities. That the less able left behind were unable to make up for the deficit amplified the effects of the catastrophe.

The systems of the slave trade worked to destroy local structures of government and social cohesion. Slave traders operated like warlords, as a law unto themselves. This disrupted existing institutions of law and order. Incentives put in place by slave traders, such as opportunities to redeem relatives sold into slavery by producing two slaves in exchange, perverted local ideas of morality and ethics.

Families on both sides of the Atlantic felt the agonies of rupture. Families and communities on the African coast and in its hinterland suffered the instability that comes with loss of group members. Nations experienced the trauma that accompanies assault on communities, families and individuals. Regions contended with the instability that results from ceaseless attack by hostile forces.

The wounds of empire to my part of the world – Southern Africa – are peculiar because they came clothed as presents. Melanated people – as we black people increasingly call ourselves – were offered the gift of modesty through clothing, the gift of knowledge through education, the gift of salvation through religion. Then there was the gift of knowledge of crime and punishment through legal systems, and the gift of speech through the coloniser's language. Each of these gifts took away something: local ideas of modesty and propriety, local knowledge systems, metaphysical and legal systems, and language. The gifts of the north-western empire to Africa were some of the most violent ones the world has known.

Such violent 'gifts' are typical of empires, not only of the Western version. The history of Ireland tells us how such imperial gifts were bestowed on white people too, in the north-west quarter of the globe, by people whose epidermis contained just as little melanin, so that the coloniser's skin colour was essentially the same hue as that of the people colonised. Empire is about power, appropriation, expropriation, and often extermination, regardless of physiology. The melanin concentration in the skin of black people was and is a convenience. It justified our ongoing subjugation even as human rights discourse germinated in the halls of world power in the United States of America, in the late 1940s, from whence it was exported to the rest of the world, just as colonial violence had been exported centuries earlier. The effect of both colonisation and human rights discourse is similar. Both make black people recipients of an imperial discourse that categorises us as wanting, and thus requiring punishment and disparagement. In its execution, the punishment is disguised as saving. We are being punished, essentially for existing and having land and resources that less melanated people would like to have, but we are not silent.

Over the centuries, Europeans gradually subjected Africa to other uses, rather than regarding the continent as merely a source of unpaid human labour. The land from which black bodies were stolen had not initially been seen as important in itself by empire. The value of the African land mass to empire lay at first in its being a source of black-embodied labour power for Western imperial agricultural industries, practised through the slave trade. The idea that the land itself was valuable developed slowly.

In Southern Africa, the Dutch started a settlement, which would become Cape Town, as a refreshment outpost on its trade route between Holland and its colony in Indonesia as early as 1652. This was a decade after the Netherlands overtook the Portuguese as the biggest African slave-trading nation, following Portuguese instigation of the practice in 1510. Although the Dutch and other Europeans began to encroach on the land occupied by Khoi-San and Bantu people immediately, frontier wars through which the Europeans wrested the land from the first nations only began over a century later in 1779. It took the Europeans another century to subdue the people of Southern Africa's coastal lands, so fierce was the resistance.

Another hundred years and more elapsed before Cecil Rhodes' British South Africa Charter Company's (BSACC's) private army, of five hundred men, armed with machine guns and other weapons, raised the British flag at the place that is present-day Harare, to annexe the land for the British empire. Colonial rule was practised through a brutal private property-based and racially exclusive patriarchy. Black men were once again valued for their labour potential in the new colonial dispensation. Now, in the days after the abolition of slavery, this labour was coerced and the remuneration for the labour was always unfair, weighted by the colonisers in their favour. The colonisers saw women and children as useless appendages to men, and grouped them together as minors before the law.

These are the wounds that burst open as I write. The force that propels my narrative through the damage is the hope not to be consumed, not to have my being rotted away, by the trauma. I write to raise mountains, hills, escarpments and rocky outcrops over the gouges in my history, my societies and their attendant spirits. The tears of the process water bushes and trees so that their roots may do the work of holding together that which was pulled violently apart. Through writing, I cultivate my being to bring forth forests that replenish our depleted humanity.

———

Empire is like a guillotine. Empire required my parents to leave their home in Southern Rhodesia to travel to London on scholarships for professional education. This education was to enable them to return to Southern Rhodesia and be even more useful to empire than they would have been without this specific imperial inculturation. The way in which they were to be useful to empire was by educating other black bodies in the ways of empire, thus delivering a new generation of bodies useful to empire.

I had no inkling that I was just a black body brought into the world only to be, in the avaricious eyes of empire, useful to it. It took a while before I could look back and see I was a baby, much as a newly born draught ox is a calf, to be broken in in due course to plough a predetermined furrow.

When my parents made the journey to England, taking me and my brother with them, I thought this was all normal life, so that normal life was as wonderful as all the surprises that amused at the beginning of the trip. Early days in England is the time when my memories begin. The time before that is without form and it is blurred. But there is light. I cannot say whether this illumination is real, the wash of subtropical sun on the pale sand of Murewa Mission, where my family lived, or whether it is the light of joy; or whether it is both, blended into a single glow of happiness; or whether I have conjured it up because I need it, a safe source. At any rate, I had not turned three at the time of the light.

In England, there was a train journey that took me to a place where the light did not follow. I do not remember that journey from Charing Cross Station in London to Dover on the south-eastern coast. Memory begins greyly with a room, whose name, I came to know, was the parlour, and they are not good memories, through no fault of the owners of the parlour. Empire was practised through them, too.

There were some very big people with my mother and father on the day I first entered the parlour. I do not remember the details, but I know that these people were pale. At the time, the colour of their skin was simply a fact, as one day I would wear a pink dress, another a green one, without connotation, and they might change the colour of their clothing, too. My dark parents and the pale parlour owners were simply all of a pattern called adults. There was quiet talk in the first room we entered. After this quiet talk in which it seemed that my brother and I were looked at with benign curiosity and much admired, we were led together into a room.

It was that room that has taught me to this day to mistrust happiness, a disposition I struggle permanently to overcome. My heart leaped so high that the world seemed to stop as I entered the parlour. It was the front room, with light, almost, although not quite as bright as my first light, pouring in from a bay window that opened on to the road. I had never experienced anything like it before. I was certain I had entered a personal wonderland: the room was full of toys painted in dazzling colours. Most of the playthings were new to me: Lego, a racetrack with cars, a rocking horse. I played with a passion that came from the absence of such toys in the two and a half years of my life until that moment. My brother and I were to play just as hard when we returned to Zimbabwe, but differently.

In Zimbabwe, when the bouts of it came upon us, our play was silent and grim, filled with neither pleasure nor gratitude, as we rode the bicycles my parents could now afford to buy us.

After a while, on the day of the parlour, one of the pale people came to fetch us. I was bursting to tell my mother and father about all the wonderful toys I had played with. Looking around, as I skipped back into the sitting room, I realised my parents were no longer there. My brother and I were told our parents were gone and we were to live here in the care of the pale people. I don't remember the words that were used, whether my brother or I, or both of us, cried or not, or if we did for how long and how we were comforted. What I remember is what I felt and it is this. I had been whole when I walked out of the parlour. A guillotine sliced through me when I walked back into the sitting room and separated many parts of me that were meant to grow increasingly whole but in that moment fled apart. I don't remember much from the days and months after that, either, which is a normal reaction to being guillotined.

After that, bedtimes were the worst. Darkness descended and something inside me started reaching out into the lightless infinity. I pulled whatever

I found there towards me. I believed the wholeness that had left when my parents did was hiding out in that unfathomable place. I wanted to reel this completeness in, to reassure myself I had not lost anything, that it was all still there so that I could reach into the never-ending emptiness, even in its horror, to reclaim what I had lost. This reaching and finding and bringing together as I lay too numb with terror to so much as tremble was the early beginnings of my writing life.

I discovered a terrible yet gratifying ease in annihilation. I was given food. I ate it without tasting it. I was carried upstairs and put to bed. I lay fearful of those things I nevertheless reached out to. They began to reciprocate, reaching back to me, and they were not what I hoped for: my parents, or at the very least, the security my parents represented. I must have cried. I know I did not sleep because soon someone sat by the bedside holding my hand for hours each night until my eyes drifted together peacefully enough to stay closed for a couple of hours. It was the beginning of my being seen as a 'difficult' child. From my perspective, the difficulty had been imposed on me, so that I was in a constant state of fear and tension, which I only amplified by trying to stare it down so that it would not smother me. My being in a permanent state of contestation made people anxious. I entered early into the conflicting dynamics of writing.

This all went on at a toddler's predominantly preverbal level. I never said, not even to myself, 'I am afraid.' I did not even know I was, but simply experienced the flow of energies. It was writing not in the sense of any verbalisation preparatory to inscription, but in the sense of striving inwardly to find the things that reduce to sense, or at least coherence, while still managing outwardly to do all the things a little Kentish girl was expected to do. I did these things with less, rather than more, success. Later, I learnt I had been fostered. Contracts had been signed between my parents and my foster family, but it made no sense and therefore did not matter.

Watching the adults around me I developed an intuitive idea that words were power. After adults spoke to each other, things happened: little children were left. My brother spoke to my foster brother and did things. The things they did together made them laugh and looked like fun. I realised I was powerless which meant I needed power, which in turn meant I needed words. With words I could do things. I could make good what was no more. Then perhaps I could bind the things that mattered to me with words and not experience their loss. I could beat the nameless things that sharpened the guillotine and came for me after I was tucked into bed. I learnt that writing begins much earlier than I was later taught to believe: that writing is no more than telling, beginning with that which you tell yourself; that the word is one method of shaping experience.

I think my foster mother understood something of the terror I experienced. She had become Mummy-Gran. She had lived through dread herself during World War II. Her husband, Granddad, was in a wheelchair because of it. She taught us Christian choruses and proceeded to talk to us about Jesus, even though I could not relate to the chubby white baby that did not even have any words of its own, but was spoken of by others. My foster mother said there were things called angels. This too was quite meaningless to me because I never saw them or heard them in the blackness that swallowed my existence each night.

At this time, I did not know that I was black. I didn't even know that I was female. I had simply possessed a certainty that I 'was' before I was set amongst the toys. Then after a time of the most exhilarating play, I learnt I could not rely on the idea that I existed just as everything else did. Most confusingly, this learning was followed by an insistence on the part of others, who had no authority to insist, who even pronounced my name wrong (Tootsie, because the first 'Tsi' was impossible to the English tongue), that I still existed. Positive emotions leave me suspicious to this day. My discoveries of who I am or who I might be are fraught with tension. The question that follows me is, 'If I discover that I am this desirable thing, will it, too, be taken away?' In other words, will I lose all sense of being again?

In the Dover foster home, I spent a lot of time on my own as my brother started school before I did. For the greater part of these periods I sat in front of the television. Here I learnt to identify frightening images such as Daleks with the ghouls in the void in the bedroom. Uplifting images, such as Millie Small singing 'My Boy Lollipop' and ballerinas drifting weightlessly across stages in white tutus signalled the pre-abandonment light. I felt my body from the outside as a thing, not from the inside as a part of me. The way I learnt that I should not touch my foster father's Daddy Henry's[2] beer glass, but could touch other glasses and pieces of pottery, is the same way I learnt that I should not touch certain parts of myself. Other parts of this body that was said to be mine, that I never experienced as such, were not out of bounds to my fingers, but annoyed me by their presence. I scratched them off, the way I poked in my dolls' pale-blue eyes. I was always sorrier once I had maimed my dolls than I was for disfiguring my own body, so that I felt awful every time I looked at the plaything's dark, hollow eye sockets in the surrounding pale-pink plastic. I did not learn to be concerned about my own body because there was no one who knew enough about what a little black girl's body looked like to notice what I had done to my own body parts. I came face to face with that little girl two decades later, when I read Toni Morrison's *The Bluest Eye*. By then, that little black girls pushed in the blue eyes of their white dolls was a knowledge I had turned my back on. Now it was written of and no one gave the verdict 'murder', and so I finally shed the secret burden of the crime of killing my white dolls by gouging out their eyes right through to their brains.

I do not remember my first school day in Dover. I take this to mean it was not particularly joyful or traumatic. On the other hand, I had become dissociated from emotion. Something that should have been vital inside me was dead. In any case, I had not seen anything alarming about my brother's experience with school and so went along to my class like any other good little girl in Kent. In fact, my brother's schooling had turned out well. He was soon smitten by his teacher, and she, I think, found him a little darling. There were many jokes and smiles, and general happiness in my foster family over my brother's *amour fou*, so that school and the falling in love that happened there seemed mostly benign. As it turned out, my teacher loathed me almost immediately. I made no friends except with a sweet boy, who I'll call Matthew. Matthew used to wonder why my skin was not the same colour as his and the rest of the class's. I had not wondered about this in my foster home. Now I began to look askance at my arms and legs.

One day Matthew said to me in all loving earnestness, 'Perhaps if I hold your hand, maybe your skin will turn white, too.' I let him hold my hand, and enjoyed the touch of another little human being, but that did not cure the new distress caused by learning some people thought I ought to be white. I pushed the anxiety to the back of my mind, and enjoyed my first love. He invited me to his birthday party. I was so excited I developed an infection that turned out to be mumps and couldn't go. The relationship ended and with no love available at school, I went down to the shed at break time to cut myself with bits of coloured glass. I had the colour of skin that white people didn't recognise lesions on. I developed a relationship with words instead. There were almost no books in my foster home. They were solid working-class people who laboured for long hours. The teacher never told me I did anything well, but by the time I was four, Mummy-Gran whipped out the newspaper when she had guests to tea to show them how well I could read.

———

My understanding of demographic categories began to burgeon at about this time. I was out with Mummy-Gran one day while she shopped, when a man smiled at me and said 'Hello, lovely little piccaninny!' In any case, I think he smiled and I think he said 'lovely' because I was elated at the greeting. I had not known what I was since my first self had been disposed of. But now I had a word for what I was: 'piccaninny'. This was firm and specific, which was comforting, or at least circumscribing: a category I could wield against the void of no longer being. I understood instinctively that the word referred to me, not to himself nor to my foster mother, much as a child understands that the word 'child' does not apply to its parents or teachers. Thus it was a word that, besides certainty, also contained in it all the creatures of the nightly void and their terrors. Since my foster family had been involved in unmaking what I had been with their toy-filled magic, I realised I should not tell any of them about the excitement I felt at my new knowledge. I waited until one of the intermittent visits my brother and I paid to our parents in London.

'Mum,' I said in a kind of triumph. 'Mum, I'm a piccaninny!'

'No, you're not,' she said in a voice that told me that even if I was not about to be cut off from her and flung back into non-existence again, the world was about to cave in.

'Piccaninny is not a good word,' she went on. 'It's a word people use to make fun of black children.'

Another identity twisted about me like a boa

constrictor. My mother's words only succeeded in confusing me further. I examined my arm to arrive at the sense of it, but ended up more puzzled. Black was the colour of the terrifying night, yet my arm didn't look like that colour to me. Still, there must be a connection I reasoned, as children do, between me and the unlit, ghoulish night. That was why the man could not just smile and call me a lovely little girl. Slowly I realised that I was linked with the colour of the malevolent darkness that terrified me every bedtime.

Practically, I had no idea black was meant to be the colour of my skin. When they absolutely had to, my foster family used the word 'coloured'. They had fostered many children from the continent. Mummy-Gran herself always referred to her charges by nationality, not by any indicator of race. Blackness is a condition imposed on me, rather than being an experienced identity. To this day, I do not identify with the word 'black' with respect to colour but with respect to experiences I have endured as a result of the imposed category.

———

Books came into my life when my family relocated to Zimbabwe, then Rhodesia. When we landed at the airport in Salisbury, as Harare was called then, in the latter part of 1965, everything appeared wrong. The buildings were too big and because of that there weren't enough people to fill them. Outside there was, to my eye, an excess of space between the buildings. The parking lot looked as large as a planet. Everything else was excessive, too: the sky too hot, bright, and blue; and too infinite, much like the night. The tarmac glinted too sharply. The air seemed too hot to breathe and shimmered with fata morganas when I looked at it. I swallowed down apprehension. Then I turned my attention to a woman who detached herself from the group of relatives who had come to meet us. She hurried back and forth in the heat, hugging my father, mother, brother, me and my sister who had been born during the family's stay in England, ceaselessly. This was the first time I did not feel anxious at meeting an unknown person. I felt love roll out from her in excited waves, and reasoned that if she embraced us all like that, she might be kind and wasn't about to tear us away from each other. I soon learnt she was my *mbuya* – my grandmother.

In the strange new world I had entered, that was said to be home – when I knew I had been given up to a home in Dover – Mbuya became my ally in no time. She watched me constantly and kindly. In a family taut with expectation, she laughed at my silly mistakes and reshaped the graver ones, by which process she introduced me to childhood. The joy that radiated from her healed, and in this way pulled down the empire within me.

The external empire posted my parents to a mission in the Eastern Highlands, near present-day Mutare City. Here, I became even more thoroughly confused concerning the category of black that was meant to indicate my skin. The mission was quite judgemental, as Christian institutions are wont to be, especially in conservative Africa. Categories were thrown up right, left and centre, over and above the old 'black'. In addition to categories such as those who drank alcohol and those who did not, those who smoked and those who didn't, there were categories of people who could or could not speak ChiVanhu.

The word ChiVanhu itself added to my confusion. Literally 'the language of the people', as opposed to, for example, Chirungu, 'the language of the white ones'. Three and a half decades earlier the imperial settler government had decreed that the name of the people in the area was Shona and their language ChiShona, but many still referred to their language as ChiVanhu and to themselves as *vanhu* – people. In conversations this led to stupefying questions such as, 'Was he a person or a European?' This in turn raised for me the pressing matter of whether or not these speakers considered *Varungu* – 'white ones/Europeans' – as people. The matter was desperately relevant to me because the tongue I spoke along with my brother – and, I believe now, due to other attributes such as our body language and way of looking – caused many of the other children to dump my brother and me in the category of *Varungu*. As a result the children didn't know what to do with us, and doubted that we could be played with like ordinary children. Yet more confusing was the fact that some American missionary children, who spoke ChiVanhu fluently, were also *Varungu*, evidenced by the fact that they did not attend the mission school, but were driven the fifteen-odd miles to town every weekday to attend the Rhodesian government's apartheid white children's school. On the other hand, a few of the missionary children went to school at the mission. The dance of my identities, of the very

44

concept of identity itself, became frenetic. 'You are an African just like everybody else,' my father said. After a while, as my language improved and my body language changed, I believed him. But secretly I was disappointed in the world. Clearly its categories were not valid.

My father brought books home from his trips, on education business, to Salisbury: Swiss Chalet and Nancy Drew for me, Hardy Boys for my brother, the Secret Seven and Famous Five for us both. I read these books alone, and never discussed them with anyone. I realised that stories order a disordered life. I only discovered my father loved stories himself when he bought a copy of *The Wind in the Willows* and read it aloud in the sitting room. He said he was reading it to my grandmother, who didn't understand a word of English, and I was too entranced by the story and my father's reading it in his wonderful voice to see through the subterfuge. The boundary between what happened in my private reading and what happened in the more public space of the family became thinner and more porous. I gave in to the pull of storytelling. In addition to reading for as many hours a day as I could, I started making up dramas for my junior school open days and organising Christmas plays with my cousins.

I enticed my younger siblings to sit and tell stories or listen to mine as often as I could. Storytelling stood in for an incomprehensible world. It gave me worlds I could cope with.

In composition class at senior school, our English teacher gave us the advice to write about what we knew in order bring it to life. O-level analyses of *Romeo and Juliet* and *Wuthering Heights* in our English literature class – theme, plot, character, conflict, climax, resolution and style – continued my education in creative writing. Ideas of rhythm and metre from our O-level poetry textbook *Adventures in Modern Verse* completed it, until I went to film school two decades later. This limited literary education was very good for me in one sense, because I thought there were very few rules. I was extremely shocked when one professor in the United States told me I wasn't in fact allowed to do what I had done in *Nervous Conditions*. And yes, he was a white man.

At the same time I learnt comforting, tidy rules of writing, I began my menses. There had been hints before that something ominous would inevitably happen: don't sit like that; don't be so strident; don't talk back like that; go and cook – these were all admonitions directed at me and not at my brother. I did not mind the doing parts of these expectations so much as the separating aspect of them. These separating aspects meant I was boxed into a category of my own where certain expectations held, while my brother wasn't included in these limitations. Once more I found myself in a dubious grouping. This category, too, threatened the injury of prejudice, while benefits like driving one of the family cars was reserved for my brother's ranking. I decided not to associate myself with the category of femaleness, with the result that I bore its consequences of doing – the dishes, the sweeping – with very bad grace. Fortunately, I did not associate looking good with femaleness, because both my parents were sharp dressers, and when my brother asked for a pair of silver Gary Glitter boots, he got them.

At school, I found out that writing could save you, but that it was also dangerous. One of my word-based ways of coping with my incompetence at living life was journalling. I had read in the British girl's magazines my mother brought back from her weekly shopping in town, that it was helpful to them for adolescent girls to keep diaries. I needed help. Our foster mother came to visit. I told her how unhappy I was. She told my mother. The silence around the subject was so dry it crumbled to powder. So I kept a diary. I took my diary to school with me. The other girls with whom I shared a dorm wanted to know what I wrote in it and didn't respect my explanation when I told them I couldn't say because a diary was private. They hunted for it and found it in its hiding place under my mattress, read it and would not let me live its contents down for months. I discovered writing could betray you. I kept reading and writing because that was all I had. There were too many energies swirling in too many parts of me – throat, heart, solar plexus, stomach; tightenings and tinglings in mind and limbs and sometimes genitals – for me not to write. I needed to fix them on paper so they would not disappear into the void from whence they might flail at me like deranged and violent apparitions, as they had done when I was young and newly guillotined. I learnt to wait until all of the energy resolved into words. Finding the word that corresponded to particular swirls was and is the only time I have known triumph or peace, and each meaningful sentence is a miracle. Gibberish lurks just beyond perception in my void. I write slowly because I must pause and be still for long enough.

Apart from poetry and fragments, I started writing

seriously at the University of Zimbabwe (UZ). I enrolled there in the early 1980s, shortly after Zimbabwe's independence. This followed a couple of years at Sidney Sussex College, Cambridge, where I was the only black woman in my college – something I had not expected given England's history of empire.

My first piece at UZ was a play called *The Lost of the Soil*, a story about a talented Zimbabwean man, John, in London in the run-up to independence. In the play, the independence movement has gathered momentum and the Zimbabwean community in John's part of London wants John to take on a leadership role. John has built up a comfortable life with his white English wife. Although he turns a blind eye to his wife's involvement in solidarity work, John refuses to do anything for the independence cause. There was not a significant black female character in this play, which reflected observations I made while I studied in England. I had visited London during the holidays, where my company was my brother's Zimbabwean friends. There were hardly any Zimbabwean women in the group. Black women were generally young and West Indian in blue-collar employment. The men around me languished in a miasma of alcohol, ganja and dub. The Zimbabweans in England who were concerned with the independence movement seemed very far from the company I kept in Cambridge. I sensed a terrible waste and destruction of potential personhood that was profoundly disturbing. Little did I know then that these young men had been constructed by empire to waste themselves in this fashion through self-anaesthesia. When I think about it now, it makes perfect sense. Destruction is the subtext of empire. It is manifest in a system that had people meant to be the nucleus of a small professional, elite middle-class send their children to be fostered in blue-collar homes. I could not escape becoming a colonial imperial subject. Therefore I became a product of an apparently benign imperial patriarchy that educated black women, but modelled them in its desired mode of 'little more than imperial male subject maintainers'. My own personhood having been stillborn, I could not project it on to paper. There was no character like me in *The Lost of the Soil*.

The ruling ZANU PF party's socialist rhetoric included, at that peri-independence moment, the liberation of women. While the legal parameters of women's emancipation were worked out in parliament, on the ground there was a moment of what looked like real class solidarity. Intellectuals, most of them white, since apart from to government that was where the money flowed, organised meetings that saw busloads of rural women transported to the capital Harare, for gatherings whose agenda was – or at least I believed was – the emancipation of all women. We didn't talk race in feminist circles in the early 1980s. Issues to do with blackness – my lack of it in some respects, and my having it in others – which were legacies of my sojourn in England as a child, receded. It was a welcome respite. Amid planning meetings, readings and discussions, I learnt the feminist methodology of flattened structures, mutual support, caregiving and of locating the personal in the political. Feminist theory showed me how I was constructed as a female person whose content and possibility was predetermined, and how my refusal to occupy that space was a form of rebellion, albeit a powerless one that simply confirmed the lack that society inscribed into me. It was at this time that I began to experience a real hunger for representation that affirmed who I was, or rather who I felt myself to be, rather than who I had been formed to be.

My new understanding of the patriarchal concept of 'lack' as a projection on to the female body, including my own, turned my focus from trying to understand men, to a concern with female emancipation and experience. The feminist slogan 'the personal is political' made it clear to me that as disempowerment occurs in community, so must reclaiming divested power have communal elements that work together with the personal. I found the fire for my writing in intersectionality, decades before I heard the term. Practically, this meant engaging, in my literary practice, with the place of the female in my society and the kinds of femaleness that I was familiar with. This process culminated in Tambudzai, the main character of *Nervous Conditions*, and the women around her. This was during the 1980s when, across the ocean, Professor Kimberlé Crenshaw,[3] a female descendant of those who had been kidnapped away, invented the term intersectionality. In terms of style, I wanted to be direct and to speak to other women in a way accessible to as many as possible.

Subject matter was easy to come by at the university. Young women went to lectures dressed up to the nines to attract male attention. Women were picked up, double-crossed and dropped as though it was the male students' rite of passage. Then there were the pregnancies. Young women in their twenties opted not to go the clinics to obtain birth control pills because of the shame attending being known to be having sex, and fear of being seen by someone who might betray them to a relative. The inevitable pregnancies occured and were much more destructive for the young women involved than for the men they slept with. *She No Longer Weeps*, my second play, was inspired by such a case. In this drama, a woman called Martha has a child while a young law student. She completes her course after giving birth, and becomes a successful lawyer who spoils her child with material possessions. Seeing Martha's success, the child's father Freddy reappears in Martha's life. Martha hires a gang of thugs to teach him a lesson and then hands herself over to the police.

Drama at the university was led by a white male South African exile, as South Arica was not, at the time, under majority rule. A black Zimbabwean man worked with him. This arrangement worked for a while. Then the black academic left, resulting in a subtle shift in power in the drama scene on campus that I found unsettling. I put a third play away before it was staged and devoted my time over many years to a manuscript that obstinately refused to resolve itself into a story in recognisable manner for a long time. This work was to become my first novel, *Nervous Conditions*.

However, if feminism gave me theory to practice by and community to practice with in the hopeful post-independence days when it seemed for a while that every sunrise was more brilliant than the previous day's, it also gave me a new struggle. White women left, money dried up, the ruling party co-opted the women's movement into its women's league. A variety of this continues still, with only those organisations sanctioned by the state receiving support, whether local or international. Feminism was branded a dirty word, leaving many, such as myself, who had flourished through feminist practice, stranded. While feminism amplified my voice, it pitted me against the mainstream.

In this environment it was difficult to publish my work as an unknown young woman writer in Zimbabwe. Of my three plays, only *She No Longer Weeps*, with its angry black woman character, which feeds into male stereotypes about (black) women, was published. *The Lost of the Soil*, which did not paint too flattering a picture of Zimbabwean masculinity, and the unproduced *The Third One*, which dealt with informal polygamy, were both rejected, even though *The Lost of the Soil*, like *She No Longer Weeps*, had played to enthusiastic audiences at the university. During a reception after the performance I received an offer to publish *The Lost of the Soil*, from an elderly, amiable white professor that I did not take up due to my fear of being trapped in the void as some abject plaything. This offer assured me that the play's later rejection was not due to its quality. The publishers then were largely young black Zimbabwean men who had left the country during the independence struggle, when their safety was at risk and opportunities were few. Now, in the early post-independence years, they had completed their education abroad and returned to the country where jobs were plentiful as white people left the newly independent former colony. While they looked down their noses at my work, they encouraged mediocrity in many aspiring women writers by whooping and applauding loudly during these aspiring women writers' readings at industry events, without offering constructive criticism. I encountered this modus operandi later on, in my career as a film-maker. In this case, mediocre black narrative was encouraged by numbers of white people in positions of power in the business.

At the time, while I was a student, I finished writing *Nervous Conditions*. The same publisher who had rejected my other two plays read and rejected the book in a condescending letter. The main objections I recall were that the book was not a novel as it wandered all over the place, and that I had conspired to make Nhamo, the protagonist's brother, horribly unsympathetic. I met the editor concerned once, by chance, after the book had become successful. I asked him what had prompted that letter and he denied having written it.

Of the three plays, only *She No Longer Weeps* is still extant. A family member who cleared out my papers burnt the other two, as well as my academic work. So little importance was attached to the art of writing.

Fortunately, by the time my papers were destroyed, the *Nervous Conditions* manuscript was sitting in the basement of a UK publishing house. Following the rejections at home, a dear friend suggested I find out where black women writers I admired were being published. These were the great African American and Caribbean female writers, Audre Lorde, Paule Marshall, Toni Morrison, Maya Angelou and Alice Walker, to name some. I am infinitely grateful that in that lacuna of time-space just after Zimbabwe's independence, I was able to access and be formed by them. I needed their voices. The pressures on me to not be myself, but to stand in for something else, continued to be immense. The university drama club was doing agit prop theatre on political themes. The government was encouraging 'revolutionary' literature that glorified the armed struggle and ZANU PF's 'victory'. Practically no one looked at the individual and the individual's experiences as worthy of attention in their own right. Even fewer, if any, were concerned with the individual personhood of young black Zimbabwean girls. Those who were interested in young black female Zimbabwean subjectivity and the representation of it in literature locked us away in the category not of 'to self-actualise' but 'to be made useful to patriarchy'. I had enthusiastically undertaken to do my bit to rectify the annihilating omission and the restricting framing. The home rejections opened my eyes further to what I was up against. I took my friend's advice. The Women's Press declared itself a feminist publishing house, and I loved the logo of a clothes iron. That was my brand of down-to-earth feminism. The fact they had published Alice Walker was another recommendation and indicated they might be open to my writing. I put the manuscript in a manila envelope and posted it across the ocean.

A manuscript from Zimbabwe did not excite, so that the package gathered dust in the publishing house's basement for several years. On a trip to London an appointment fell through, leaving me with some time on my hands. I debated whether to go over to the Women's Press offices or not. I was reluctant to face being turned down yet again. On posting the manuscript, I'd told myself that if it didn't work, I'd give up writing altogether. In spite of such gloomy thoughts, something stronger than fear pushed me to the publishing house's address. I'd grown used to fear from my experience with the guillotine and the void. I knew fear was ubiquitous and the trick was to keep it a hair's breadth away. It is what I interpret Toni Morrison as meaning when she writes about a character keeping very still. So I kept very still, walked down the street and knocked at the door. After I'd made my enquiry, I was assured that if I had indeed sent a manuscript, and it had arrived, it would be in the basement. The woman who assured me of this disappeared down a flight of stairs. After I had waited for a few anxious minutes, she reappeared blowing dust and cobwebs from the package I had posted.

Providence in the form of empire – or rather resistance against it – led me to the publisher, the late Ros de Lanerolle at the Women's Press. Ros was a South African exile who lived in London at the time, who immediately recognised the story I wrote of a young village girl called Tambudzai Sigauke, who, coming from an impoverished family, fights for an education because she thinks that this will be her route to a better life. It was with the publication of *Nervous Conditions* that I understood what it meant to write while black, as well as being female. Being categorised as black and female does not constrain my writing. Writing assures me that I am more than merely blackness and femaleness. Writing assures me I am. What writing while black and female does constrain for me is access to publication opportunities, and when I am published, avenues to reputable, professional publishing houses and lucrative contracts, money being the currency of empire.

I had already given up on a literary career by the time that *Nervous Conditions* was published, and had turned into the black African woman's narrower, nastier – which I thankfully did not know at the time – cul-de-sac of film-making, As there was no film school in Zimbabwe I was obliged to train abroad and was delighted at being accepted into the German Film and Television Academy Berlin, which was then a very prestigious school. My writing became screenwriting and again – with the exception of a few of our trainers, mainly the ones from Eastern Europe – I discerned an impenetrable lack of interest in my subject matter: the emancipation and experiences of black African women. Daily, until today, I bashed my head against a wall of wilful refusal to admit my realm of experience into imagination and thence into visual narrative. I continued my training only due to the support of another African student, Wanjiru Kinyanjui from Kenya. Wanjiru sat with me on my birthday, organised crews for my shoots and had my back at every turn, support that continues to this day. Finally a new director was appointed and the climate at the school changed for the better for me. Beyond film school, I began to be invited to write full-length scripts, for white men and women making films about Zimbabwe and other parts of Africa. These films went on to receive production funding and enjoyed some success, while my own scripts have not been afforded the same resources. One of my scripts, *Dear Nnenna*, a coming-of-age high-school drama, adapted from a popular Nigerian novel and workshopped with young writers, has a budget of

US $285,000. But this is too much money for those people who have given white people making films in my part of the world many hundreds of thousands of dollars. My dark comedy, *Q-ing*, a musical about trying to obtain fuel during a chronic fuel shortage in a police state, has been sitting around for decades. Then there's the story about a young man from a wealthy Asian South African family who discovers his mother is the maid. And the list goes on.

Meanwhile, increasing numbers of young black women from the continent were published. Notwithstanding, on the literary circuit in the 1990s at events to which I travelled from Berlin, I heard doleful women joking about a renewed difficulty of publication: *They've already got a black one*. It now turns out that the 'black one' who had already been contracted was usually from a group of certain African nations; namely from three of Great Britain's former colonies where English is an official language – the states of Nigeria, South Africa and Kenya. This is in some part due to globalisation. Companies look to make profits, as profit is most easily realised when familiar characters are presented, yet familiarity itself is bolstered by a steady supply of narrative. These three countries have incorporated the creative industries into their economic models and are building up literary, as well as other arts traditions. The African arts triangle effect is strongest in the film sector. In Zimbabwe, on the other hand, literary accomplishment has declined with the decline in education during the militarised ZANU PF's immiseration strategy of power retention, under which any pretence of supporting the arts has come to an end. In addition to coming from the wrong country, I was also beginning to suffer from another debilitating demographic: age. Added to all this, I did not have an agent, the Women's Press owed me money when they floundered, which was never paid, and my new publisher did not treat me in the professional manner in which I expected to be treated. It looked like it was too late to change this.

Stifled by the inability of gatekeepers to perceive me as a competent film-maker and my protagonists as competent subjects, I returned to Zimbabwe, where I could centre myself again. I was now married, with two small children, soon to be three. It was the turn of the millennium. The political landscape in Zimbabwe had deteriorated. Signs of autocracy and the denial of human beings' fundamental rights were already apparent to those who knew where to look, and after my long break from home, I did. There was no question of my sitting down to the long and intense unpaid labour that for me characterised writing, whether it was prose or for the screen. I ended up joining an NGO, Women Filmmakers of Zimbabwe, which enabled me to eke out a living through founding a women's film festival, the International Images Film Festival for Women.

These are not years I like to remember, even with the publication in 2006 of my second novel, *The Book of Not*, which is a sequel to *Nervous Conditions*, by Ayebia Clarke.

A decade after founding the women's film festival, the organisation received a three-year grant that enabled me to plan growth and follow through. Once I had established functioning systems in the office with the grant, I was able to focus on the manuscript that would become *This Mournable Body*. The spectre of rejection jeered at me from the void yet again, until the indomitable Zimbabwean-born editor Ellah Wakatama Allfrey took the book under her wing pro bono and found the book's United States publisher. The two of us turned out to be the community I needed, just as the feminist community had brought me to the place within myself where I could hear my own voice. *This Mournable Body* was published in 2018 by Greywolf Press in the US and then shortlisted for the 2020 Booker Prize after publication by Faber in the UK.

The book received excellent reviews from most corners of the former empire, from both men and women. The two worst reviews I received were from white men at the heart of empire, writing for *The Times* and the *Daily Telegraph*. *The New Statesman* showed restraint by calling me extraordinary and focusing on that label, rather than the writing in the book under review. Even though writing while black and female does not constrain my writing process, it does position my writing's content. I write from my personhood, scattered as it is across continents and within voids. Through words I raise the blade of the guillotine, reach for the dismembered parts, and rejoin them to the rest of my being, while the monster of empire practised through patriarchy snaps at my heels.

Black, Female and the Superwoman
Black Feminist

Long before female superheroes became fashionable, I had created my own. She was twenty metres tall. Her skin was the colour of copper. She wore her hair in plaited extensions, in a long ponytail that trailed down her back. My female superhero strode over huts and houses. She kicked away snakes that were about to bite children, pulled livestock out of ravines and snapped up between her finger and thumb men who practised violence on the bodies and souls of women, after which she flung the unfortunate beings to the horizon. Who wouldn't be afraid of her?

I needed a superhero for the same reason everyone else does – to manage anxiety about a relentlessly terrifying humanity. Patriarchy was my first manmade terror, following the existential problem of being on the planet at all. I learnt early how the males of our species gang up against people they judge as being weaker, especially if they feel they have already been vanquished by the society they find themselves living in.

The lessons came from my biological brother and from my foster brother, who teased me mercilessly. My foster brother was several years older than my brother and me. Working through his own separation anxieties, my brother bonded with this older male, with whom he wrestled and to whom he looked up in our two-up, two-down home that housed three generations of my foster family, plus foster children. One day, when I had had enough of my foster brother tormenting me, I squealed. My foster father, a man I called Daddy Henry, slapped my foster brother, his son, about the head. That made two of us cry. As far as I could see, male energy didn't have any good uses. No matter what they did, men had a knack of making you feel bad. I was an infant adversary of toxic masculinity at the age of three.

Two years later I rejoined my biological parents in London for a transitional period before the family returned to Zimbabwe, then called Rhodesia. Dad took us children to the movies, but even as we rode up and down in the Tube, the shadow of his rage should something go wrong, like losing my ticket, loomed over the excitement of the outing. This rage wasn't only directed at me: it could erupt toward anyone in range who was a close enough relative to my father to offer a safe target. My brother identified with Dad, as he had done with my foster brother, and even offered Dad, once, the means of punishing me by handing over his little belt. I suspect he did this to relieve his own feelings of powerlessness. My contempt for society's construction of maleness as a mode of being that requires hurtful power over others for validation, devoid of compassion, even for its own pain, was established early.

Back in Zimbabwe, I could not understand why male energy was privileged, as though it vibrated at a higher frequency, leading to my brothers receiving entitlements which I, along with my younger sister, did not enjoy. There was, nevertheless, a certain degree of feminist ethic in my childhood environment that bolstered my critical thinking. We children had routine chores to do in the house and yard. My father was fond of having us wash up, pointing out that we and the domestic help were equal where human dignity was concerned, so that just as we appreciated their assistance, the help would appreciate us supporting them. Dad apportioned his tasks without regard to sex. My brother and I both did washing up and worked in the fields and garden. My mother, though, policed my femininity with a vengeance. I helped with cleaning the house, laundering, ironing and sweeping the yard. The vigilante in her oversaw privileges, too: my brother went mountain climbing with other young people, drove the family car and spent days in Mutare, while I didn't, with most of the permissions being granted or withheld by parental consensus. I decided on subversion which led to ongoing efforts – mostly unsuccessful – to boycott the things my brother was not made to do. Having earlier been called a difficult child, I now graduated to fractious adolescent.

———

By the time I was in my teens, I had taken up an existence framed by a double negative: not male, not white. Not male came with other 'nots': not kind, not benign, not smiling. This meant instead of deploying my energy to positive effect, I was constantly pushing back against negatives. Continually engaging with negativity was disorienting and made me nervous. I felt badly off-centre. Racism didn't describe it all, in spite of Ian Smith's settler government inclining increasingly toward an apartheid system similar to the one that was in place in South Africa at the time. The settler government's policies had thrown the country into a civil war that pitted the colonial regime against black nationalists and the handful of white and other groupings who supported the principle of majority rule. The guerrillas, trained in the communist bloc, drummed the doctrine of class struggle into the people. However, class struggle did not account for the viciously sexualised attacks upon members of the population they were said to be trying to free. Nor did class struggle account for the sexual abuse of women in the guerrilla camps. Only a few women who had been active in the guerrilla ranks were brave enough to speak out after the war ended. I didn't find a word that accounted for the workings of what I called maleness until I was in my early twenties as a student at the University of Zimbabwe (UZ). It was there, thanks to a group of older women, mainly white and expatriate, that I came across the word 'patriarchy'.

The time was the 1980s, a couple of years after Zimbabwe's independence. Independence had been gained in 1980 after a guerrilla war that lasted one and a half decades. The war was prosecuted by black Zimbabwean nationalist movements that, in the early 1960s, split into two groups roughly aligned with the two major ethnic groups in the country: Shona and Ndebele. The Shona grouping is the larger, population-wise, which led to its nationalist political party the Zimbabwe African National Union – Patriotic Front (ZANU PF) obtaining a majority at the elections that followed peace negotiations at Lancaster House in London. In reality there was no great division between the political and military wings of the nationalist ZANU PF machinery, which was a military movement and government-in-waiting in exile. On being elected to power, the guerrilla movement turned ruling political party made a raft of social reforms to cement its image as a new example for Africa.

The reforms included the 1982 Legal Age of Majority Act or LAMA, under which black women in Zimbabwe were legally emancipated at the age of eighteen, to become, in law at least, the equal of black men. This piece of legislation was revolutionary. Up until LAMA was passed, African women in Zimbabwe had been perpetual minors under codified law. Even after she reached the age of twenty-one, an African woman remained subordinate to her male guardian, unable to enter into any contracts, employment or marriage without the written permission of this male guardian. That meant she could not earn money to sustain herself through formal employment, could not own land or start her own business without her male guardian's consent. Even medical decisions, such as tubal ligation, were made by male guardians. My *Nervous Conditions* character, the postgrad-educated Maiguru, is an example of how the need to adapt themselves to these kinds of restrictions eroded an African woman's sense of agency and selfhood, with the result that many African women often reflected a distorted sense of womanhood and female power to themselves, and to female and male members of their families, as well as to their communities. The effect of imperial colonial legislation was to lump African women together as undifferentiated adjuncts to humanity, characterised by inferiority to men.

Educated in South Africa at Fort Hare University and at King's College, London, my mother was the first black woman in Southern Rhodesia to obtain a bachelor's degree. My mother was, as I often am too, for better or worse, a first. She then went on to do her master's at University College London, majoring in English and Latin. Returning to Rhodesia after the British settlers in the country had declared unilateral independence from Great Britain in 1965, she was an inspiring role model for the young women she taught. At her death her old students banded together to sing her praises and to give eulogy after eulogy, about how my mother had taught them a viable, achieving kind of womanhood. Professionally she was the kind of teacher who had the young men in her classes speaking Latin in the school corridors. That was her personal power. But I suspect she never fully enjoyed the achievement society allowed her, because she knew she could have been so much more, that the true extent of her personal power was limited by a history and present that positioned African women in a disempowered space throughout the colonial era.

This constraining positioning of black African women was practised in all the British Empire's African colonies. Britannica.com describes Theophilus Shepstone, the man who devised this system of degrading the humanity of African women, even more than that of their men, as a 'British official in Southern Africa who devised a system of administering Africans on which all later European field administrations in Africa were to be based'. Brought up in the Cape and educated at his father's mission school there, Shepstone moved to Natal in the mid-nineteenth century when he took up the first of several posts in the British colonial government. Shepstone was a consummate apartheidist on the grounds that black people were unfit to take part in white society until they were properly civilised. Engaging with the 'unfit to take part' proposition of his belief, rather than notion of civilising, problematic in itself, Shepstone concluded that a system of indirect rule needed to be established. He set about negotiating with indigenous authorities with the intention of rendering these tribal powers useful to the colonisation effort, often through the ruse of playing one off against the other. Two of his enduring legacies include reserves on which Africans lived, and the codification of the local customs of the time as law through dialogue exclusively with men. Through the latter, African women's subjectivity was simply expunged from colonial discourse and practice. This second of colonial rule's divide-and-rule strategies was gendered. African men were pitted against African women and identified with the encroaching colonial force, even though time would soon show that this identification would not save them from their own abject subjugation by the settlers. So successful were Shepstone's strategies, including his gender strategies, in subverting local power in the interests of empire that the model went on to be used in all British colonies in Africa.

Shepstone's codes are what came to be called 'traditional' or 'customary' law, although they were little more than a set of normative practices as envisioned by the men he spoke to at the time that the conversations took place. Thus they reflected the concerns and desires of the moment. Local law was neither codified nor legislated. It existed through normative custom, and was regulated by the incumbent monarch at any given time. In this way local legal practices were flexible enough to accommodate changing contexts. Through Shepstone's intervention, African women were frozen into a moment in the nineteenth century as imagined and narrated through the eyes of black and white men, a moment that saw them as fit only for subjugation.

The local traditional systems had been patri-archal. However, this traditional patriarchy was built on kinship, a foundation that made it qualitatively different from patriarchal systems that are anchored in private ownership. Ownership implies an object to be possessed, and a possessor who possesses it. Objects in private ownership need to be quantifiable as they require to be counted. Thus ownership is a system of disaggregation and control as precursors to a central act of acquisition. These precursors render strife and conflict, presented as competition, fundamental in any system (including patriarchal systems) based on private ownership.

On the other hand, systems of patriarchy grounded in kinship acknowledge the infinite nature of relational bonds, and the need to ensure the continuance of these bonds through proper access to resources by everyone. This is why pre-colonial society dealt harshly with individuals said to interfere with the stability of these bonds through practices such as witchcraft. By disrupting positive bonds in society, witchcraft was a threat to social cohesion. Pre-colonial patriarchy was not utopian, as many Africans are inclined to believe, but due to its ideological genesis, it afforded space to and conferred respect on female power: women were kinspeople whose power was to be valued.

Accordingly, traditional patriarchy recognised differing degrees and locations of female power. In my part of the world, female power was and still is practised through the male line. A paternal aunt wields power in the extended family that can be regarded as 'female fatherhood', even when her status in the family she marries into is the lowly condition of *muroora*, daughter-in-law – literally the one who is married. Critically, women were not absolutely deprived of power as kinship systems of patriarchy ensured that everyone had power in some capacity. Hence women could and did become rulers and warriors, and royal spirit mediums called *mhondoro*.

One of the most famous *mhondoro* is the woman Charwe. Charwe was a spirit medium in the Mazowe Valley area of Zimbabwe, which is some eighty kilometres north of Harare. She was said to become possessed by the spirit of Nehanda, who had co-founded the Mutapa dynasty along with her brother in the fifteenth century. In 1896, Charwe organised a rebellion against the increasingly oppressive British South Africa Company, one of Cecil Rhodes' private companies, that ruled the area. A particularly tyrannical native commissioner called H. H. Pollard was killed during the rebellion. The company sent its police force to hunt Charwe down. She was captured and hanged in 1897.

With locations of power and influence assured to them, the idea of women in Zimbabwean and many other African settings fighting for power was as absurd as it was an abomination. African philosophy did not proscribe women's access to power, but through the philosophy of *ubuntu* whose central tenet is 'I am because you are', peace was highly valued and members of communities were expected to practice it, rather than fight each other. Only those who were designated as 'not I and not you', which is to say 'not we', could legitimately be engaged in combat. As anyone who approached in peace became a 'you-who-I-am', the notion of 'we' expanded to be inclusive. In the pre-capitalist agrarian societies of African traditional community, women had little incentive to fight for power as a group.

This had all changed by the time my mother was born in the 1920s. In 1899, Cecil Rhodes' company created a legislative council which effectively turned its territories into a self-governing colony. Across the seas in London, however, British courts ruled that all land that was not privately owned belonged to the

British Crown. This ruling entrusted the settlers with responsible government of all the new colony's land, and its inhabitants. Africans pushed for independence first by peaceful political means, and when these were spurned, through an armed struggle that lasted from 1966 to 1979, ending in a ZANU PF government. Life under this guerrilla-turned-lawmaker government presented dismaying inconsistencies early on in my young feminist days.

Very shortly after the legislation conferring majority status came into law, news of atrocities being carried out there began to filter through from Matabeleland. It was hard to reconcile the progressive legislation the government enacted with rumours of genocide. Factual information disconfirming or confirming the rumours was practically impossible to obtain as there was a complete blackout in the media – print, television and radio – which were all state-owned. The rumours of atrocities in Matabeleland combined with hushed reports of similar atrocities that these same people had committed during the war, told in small family circles by victims and eyewitnesses, were gradually repeated in widening circles. Simultaneously, ZANU PF began its campaign to nationalise feminism by rolling its Women's League out through the nation. Women who had danced and sung, 'Oh, Mr Mugabe, I want to strap you to my back,' when ZANU PF returned from the Lancaster House conference proclaiming a triumphant military victory were now harnessed to prop up the ruling party through its feminine structures. The celebratory climate of early independence soon came to an end. The feminist meetings at the University of Zimbabwe that had so informed my germinal feminism soon came to a stop too. White expatriate feminist women left the country. Then, to our dismay, in 1999, less than two decades after its promulgation, the Supreme Court attacked the provisions of the Legal Age of Majority Act.

The attack was made in the infamous case of *Magaya v. Magaya*. In 1990, only eight years after it had passed LAMA, ZANU PF went on to pass the Customary Law and Local Courts Act, which harked backed to Shepstone's positioning of African women. This Act established a new variety of court, called a community court, in order to apply customary law in rural areas, now called communal lands. These were the reserves that Shepstone had created. By the time the *Magaya v. Magaya* case came before courts, the Act had already been amended two years previously. Simon Coldham has this to say about the case:

The issue before the court was deceptively simple: when an African male has died intestate, leaving a daughter (his eldest child) by his first marriage and three sons by his second marriage, who is entitled to be appointed heir to his estate? In this case the Community Court had held that the daughter (the appellant) was not entitled to be appointed heir, given that there was a son able to act, and it awarded the heirship to the second son (the respondent), the eldest son having disclaimed it. The daughter appealed to the Supreme Court, challenging the appointment. The appeal was dismissed.

Under section 68(1) of the Administration of Estates Act, the applicable law at the time, the deceased's estate fell to 'be administered and distributed according to the customs and usages of the tribe or people to which he belonged'. After referring to a number of court decisions as well as two books on African Customary Law, the Supreme Court concluded that an heir succeeded to the status of the deceased, inheriting both rights and responsibilities, and that, in the appointment of heirs, males were preferred to females. The Court then had to address the question whether this discriminatory principle of customary law should either be struck down as unconstitutional or be held to be inconsistent with the Legal Age of Majority Act.[1]

Several previous decisions that had eroded Zimbabwean women's rights were cited by the Supreme Court in coming to its decision. The arguments in the *Magaya v. Magaya* case are telling. In dismissing the eldest's appeal to be appointed heir to her father's estate, the 1999 Zimbabwean Supreme Court reasoned that women were discriminated against in inheritance matters not because of an irreversible minority status but because the notion of minority was Western and therefore inapplicable in a traditional setting. The court opined that 'the reason why men were preferred as heirs was not because women were "perpetual minors", but because on marriage women would leave the family of their birth and join their husband's family. The Legal Age of Majority Act was designed "to remove disabilities rather than to confer rights"',[2] and it was therefore irrelevant in the customary setting. A poor woman who was unable to prove emancipation – and therefore qualification to be tried under

Roman-Dutch Law – was discriminated against by the ruling.

Section 23 of the Constitution of Zimbabwe at the time of the case did provide protection from discrimination. However, this protection only extended to discrimination resulting from 'race, tribe, place of origin, political opinions, colour or creed'. In spite of the 1982 LAMA conferring majority status on African women, discrimination based on sex remained legal. Other areas in which discrimination on the basis of sex remained legal were in the areas of adoption, marriage, divorce and burial. The source of this discrimination in private ownership of property was evidenced by the failure of the then Constitution of Zimbabwe to provide protection with respect to matters of devolution of property on death, or other matters of personal law, and the application of African customary law in any such case involving Africans.

The Supreme Court's decision, as well as the previous discriminatory decisions on which it relied, emphasised the performative nature of the seemingly enlightened work of the Zimbabwean state. In 1980 Zimbabwe was a new nation state, with the eyes of the world looking towards it. Progressive legislation evoked goodwill towards the new republic. However, the changes were cosmetic. Performative progressive actions were such a staple of the new nation's patriarchy that feminists needed to be on constant high alert, exhibiting the hypervigilance that is today also a condition of black people in racialised societies. Some actions carried out ostensibly to address gender inequality were downright regressive. After independence, Zimbabwean citizenship laws provided that children born to Zimbabwean fathers were citizens by descent, regardless of the country of birth. This birthright was not extended to the children of Zimbabwean mothers. When women's rights groups lobbied for the law to be amended, the birthright was rescinded in the case of children born to Zimbabwean fathers, rather than extended to children born to Zimbabwean mothers. This situation prevailed until the 2013 constitutional amendment. This amendment was the result of a contested election that saw the ZANU PF party form a government of national unity with the Movement for Democratic Change.

Women experience gendered and sexualised trauma every day. A man stretches out his hand to touch your breasts while you walk down the street.

There is nowhere to report the violation of privacy. A woman is stripped for wearing a miniskirt or even tight trousers. She's too traumatised to think of reporting it and certainly doesn't want to face more men. A woman is abused during a medical examination. The Medical and Dental Council of Zimbabwe says it never received her letter of complaint when she follows up. Women on campus are seized by the subtle, unnamed fear of rendering themselves unmarriageable through excessive learning. Sexual relationships based on gratitude and terror lead to unplanned pregnancies that result in the expecting female student needing to catch up work missed when she returns after having her baby. The daunting prospect of extra academic work while caring for an infant results in many women not returning at all. There is no woman-friendly recourse for women in such straits.

Zimbabwean patriarchy has long been particularly reluctant to recognise the achievement of Zimbabwean women in any sector that it does not control. I am no longer surprised by this as I have observed that members of oppressive classes are more disposed to oppress the members of a category that is close to themselves than they are to oppress members of categories that are very different. Thus Africans will oppress each other and elevate European or Chinese people. Zimbabwean men will recognise women who are not Zimbabwean, but rarely Zimbabwean women.

As a young feminist at the UZ, I had unlearnt the lessons of my teenage years: that females were supposed to put up with not being accommodated and that failing to do so made a woman unpopular. Instead of being wary of other black feminist women, I made friends with one of the lecturers in the Faculty of Social Sciences. As a feminist herself, and as a sociologist who had distinguished herself through influential feminist analysis of Zimbabwean literature, my friend was interested in my work as a playwright because it gave voice to gendered perspectives. As the Zimbabwean government was still performing Marxism at the time, it gave a degree of support to some local arts institutions, particularly events likely to raise its international profile, such as festivals. This led to the ZANU PF government supporting the Zimbabwe International Book Fair, ZIBF, which at that time was the largest book fair in Southern Africa.

In the run-up to the book fair in 1984, a report in the state newspaper announced that the book fair would feature female writers. My friend and I waited to receive our invitations. They did not come. Leaning in, we wrote a letter to the editor, demanding an explanation for why women writers from abroad were deemed newsworthy while Zimbabwean women writers were not, and also asking the book fair to explain its exclusion of local women writers. Repression, regression and Zanuism along with its Women's League-supported state patriarchy were not as absolute then as they have become today. The letter was published. My friend, whose profile as a respected lecturer in sociology was higher than mine, was, at the last minute, invited to participate.

Such small victories bolstered my belief in the efficacy of active feminist sisterhood at the personal level, and the power of feminism to effect change in the community in a more general way. Going forward, nevertheless, it was easy for the writers who managed the book fair to punish me by ignoring me further, with my first attendance as an invited guest taking place during a special women's edition in 1999, more than ten years after I had become an internationally recognised fiction writer.

A few years later, I founded and ran, for a decade and a half, a women's film festival. It was called the

International Images Film Festival for Women. It was to screen films with female protagonists so that women could see themselves magnified to giant proportions pursuing their womanly goals up on the screen. The cultural attaché at a European country's embassy, who supported the festival at the time, cautioned me against expecting too much success for the festival as men still controlled the industry, as well as everything else, and despised the efforts of women to stake claims in male-dominated areas. That was a white feminist speaking. What of black African feminists? While marginalisation by patri-archal structures and lack of access to resources and sustainable livelihoods that is constructed by patri-archy is true for the majority of women, it is much truer for feminists; and among feminists it is more true for feminists who live and work in disadvan-taged environments such as those that many black feminists work in in Africa.

The situation has changed in some measure. For example, in Zimbabwe, the discriminatory clauses of the Constitution of Zimbabwe have been superseded by the provisions of the Constitution of Zimbabwe Amendment (No. 20) Act , 2013, but black feminists in Africa continue to be a small, often embattled group. Fear of repercussions, such as being disciplined in one form or another or being ostracised, still keeps many women from claiming, or even desiring power. Outside of the international NGO community, which continues to fund some highly selective feminist activities, young black women on the continent are reluctant to call themselves feminist even when they make the intellectual connections between power and gender on the one hand, and freedom, access and reward on the other. Being a feminist of conviction while black and female, as opposed to a career or NGO feminist, is to live constantly at the brink of survival. Our existence is not supported by our environments. We have to work hard for moments of affirmation, where we can experience feminist community, power, lightness and joy.

Accordingly, such moments of regeneration and community do not occur frequently for us feminists on our African continent. When they do, they are generally in the context of a development agenda, not in the context of the personal lives and well-being of women from different walks of life. Circumstance and struggle are reduced to ticks in boxes, regardless of lived experience. When couched in global north–south development objectives, feminism takes on a post-colonial liberal position that encourages patri-archal governments to create policy papers on inclusion without incentives for implementation, rendering them nothing more than administrative performances. The nature of each individual woman's struggle remains untouched, unless they are women involved in NGO programmes sanctioned by government.

The marginalisation of feminists extends to economic exclusion. Their workplaces are under-resourced. Husbands forbid their wives to take jobs in organisations perceived as feminist. While global feminism has developed doctrines of self-care, this is often beyond the economic means of most black African feminist women who are commonly the only or an equal co-breadwinner in a family. Being stretched beyond endurance, many burn out and give up or simply emigrate. Their praxis continues in foreign lands, while inside the country the captured women's institutions, bolstered by government income which includes aid packages, become the de facto women's movement. In spite of women's legal status, women continue to be con-figured by society, including themselves, as assets to be acquired by masculine community for masculine fulfilment. It is understood by both groups that these female-embodied assets are acquired by male-embodied individuals solely in order to augment the experience and performance of often nationalist, always patriarchal masculinities.

While I continue to experience isolated instances of backlash, particularly when I aspire to power and influence – such as when I aspired to be president of the Zimbabwe Film Development Platform, which I had founded in 2016, after spending a term as its deputy – my age insulates me from the most atrocious forms of Zimbabwean misogyny. These include sex for work, child sexual abuse and child marriages. Most affected are young women, who are still building their lives. Their environment offers them little.

Zimbabwe is a country with practically no middle class. It has never had one. A racial elite was built up under British colonial rule and under subsequent British settler rule. This social engineering was continued when the settlers unilaterally declared independence from Great Britain in 1965. At this time the settler government, which lasted until 1979, embarked on a strategy to create a black middle class to act as a buffer against the millions of Zimbabweans who had been relegated to the quasi-humanity, reminiscent of the 'black cattle' that Reni Eddo-Lodge[3] reminds us were a staple of the transatlantic slave trade. The majority black population was relocated to reserves, in a system that had first been experimented with by the eighteenth-century British colonial administrator, Theophilus Shepstone, in Natal, South Africa.

The efforts to create an economic middle class where only a racial elite class had existed before, were an eleventh-hour effort to save a white supremacy threatened by the nationalist guerrilla war that was waged throughout the 1970s. This attempt failed with Zimbabwe's independence in 1980 and the advent of a majority government. Into this failure stepped ZANU PF with its militarised mafia patriarchy. As non-state feminist actors continue to observe, it soon became clear that the party's women's wing had nothing to do with women's emancipation, but was another battalion in the Zimbabwean state's militarised repressive machinery. The women's wing's job was to support the status quo and carry out orders without question. Maternal mortality and childhood malnutrition, including death from malnutrition, have increased dramatically in the last few years, without a word from this women's wing. In July 2020, seven babies died in one day at one of the country's largest referral hospitals due to Covid-19-related staffing issues. The mothers in the ZANU PF women's wing were silent. In August 2021, a fourteen-year-old girl whose family belongs to one of the many quasi-Christian religious sects that regularly spring up in the country was raped, resulting in a pregnancy. Complications set in during delivery. As the sect does not permit medical treatment, she was taken to a shrine but subsequently died. Through it all the women's league remained mute. These sects, because of their numbers and authoritarian structures that allow their leaders to determine for whom followers vote, have been courted by successive ZANU PF governments. Elite women quietly enjoy the privileges of patriarchy, knowing that their elite status could be revoked at any moment.

The truth is, no woman is safe from ZANU PF's predatory patriarchy. Politically motivated acts of violence against women are on the increase. Three women youth leaders from the opposition party, the Movement for Democratic Change (MDC), have been persecuted relentlessly since early in 2020 for their political activity. The young women allege they were abducted and tortured by state agents following an arrest in which they were not charged but secreted away from the police station. The alleged torture included being made to ingest their waste matter. On returning to the police station to report the alleged crime, they were charged with the criminal offence of faking an abduction. Tweets from high-level government officials variously accused them of having faked their torture or of attending a lover's tryst that went wrong.

The misogyny that feminists fight in Zimbabwe is so normalised that not even elite women are spared when they dare to go against the mainstream, but are severely punished in the country's conservative society. Grace Mugabe, wife of the late Robert Mugabe who ruled over Zimbabwe like a monarch for nearly four decades through the ZANU PF party, became the cause of her family's downfall after she reached out for power to keep political power in her aged husband's faction, even though she neither identified as a feminist, nor acted in any manner that could be construed as feminist. Seeing women elevated to privilege through marriage to a powerful man, only to crash violently once the relationship to the man ends, is a potent signal to Zimbabwean women to stay in line. The fate of Marry Mubaiwa, former common-law wife of Zimbabwe's vice-president in today's military rulership, is another terrifying warning to all Zimbabwean women. Following the break-up of the marriage she is before the courts on charges of, amongst others, having slapped a domestic worker and having conspired to solemnise her common-law marriage to her husband without his permission. The various charges read like a soap opera, making the fact that they are being pursued at the highest levels of Zimbabwean power all the more chilling. Although Ms Mubaiwa is seriously ill, she is not allowed to travel out of the country for treatment and her access to treatment in Zimbabwe is hindered through financial constraints imposed on her bank accounts. In November 2021, the courts ordered her imprisonment for ten days to allow the state to determine whether or not she was fit to stand trial. Feminists in the country released a statement urging the state not to use the courts to settle scores in divorce wrangles and expressing their concern for Marry Mubaiwa's life, but there is little more that feminists – beleaguered, starved of resources and influence, and working within weak institutions most of which do not survive the pressures they face – can do. To be a feminist while black and female in Zimbabwe is to live at the epicentre of structural racism and a brutal militarised patriarchy that has co-opted significant state institutions either in part or in their entirety.

Certain women are elevated to privilege in our patriarchal societies. These are the ones who conform to their subordination. The mechanism works at all levels of society. Elite women are often used as examples for the rest of female society as to how women should acquiesce to gendered constructions of power, the argument being that a woman can still be successful from a position of subordination to men. In Zimbabwe some women continue the traditional practice of curtseying or kneeling before their husbands, a practice I call marital genuflection. Powerful women are quoted in the media, claiming that although they have elevated socio-economic positions, they still perform marital genuflection, cook, clean, fetch and carry for their husbands in the privacy of their homes. And indeed, it is women who are likely to make such claims who are elevated to privilege by our societies.

Far be it from me to decry women who perform acts of domestic labour as a love offering. There are men for whom such acts are a love language, too, albeit few and far between. My concern is with performances of subservience as a normative practice based on gender power relations, where such acts become not expressions of personal connection but of societal control. With respect to marital genu-flection, I strongly believe that any human being who requires or permits another human being to kneel before them has deeply suspicious motives and a human being who finds it normal habitually to kneel to a fellow human being needs saving.

Beside the overt message, these women send other subtle messages to the women who watch them, and who aspire to be as successful as they are. A woman's career achievement is de-normalised and rendered atypical. It is constructed as an event that has to be atoned for. The achieving woman must prove that she is still feminine, or, as it is put locally, 'wife material'. Women are required to confirm that their success is within the framework of a patriarchal agenda, and will not destabilise it. It is a kind of quid pro quo. The subtext of the women's assertions is, 'In spite of my defiance of patriarchy in that way, I still concede to patriarchy in this way.' This kind of silencing of women's ambition works together with the exclusion of African feminists from work, and thus from sustainability and thriving and flourishing. It is a far-reaching tactic of our societies. Work is creative. Work produces. Effort that does not produce for the one who expends the effort is not work. It is slavery.

Work is a manifestation of power. Work is impossible where there is no power. Exclusion from work results in self-attributions by women, including many feminist women so affected, of lack of power.

Zimbabwean women, in a country where every civil index from the economy to democratic space is shrinking, are made to understand the not-so-subtle threat of being categorised adversely and being left to fend for themselves in an increasingly brutal economic environment.

A complementary strategy is manufactured muting and invisibility. Successful women in conservative Zimbabwean society, and other African societies who are not constrained in their private and public lives by woman-unfriendly norms, are muted by a patriarchal media. At the same time, the same patriarchal structures, and the intersection of these patriarchal structures with international liberal structures, work to ensure that there is no women's media. Conversely, women who are emancipated in both their public and private lives choose not to talk about their emancipation. Reasons range from a desire to protect precious privacy to fear of reprisals, not least having the husband who tolerates such behaviour ridiculed. There are increasing numbers of such progressive men, as a result of the work that feminists have done over the decades, but there again, silence renders most of them invisible. Fear of reprisals also prompts such women to dissociate themselves from feminism, reinforcing the perception of feminism as a pernicious cult, and feminists as bands of detestables. In the absence of a dedicated conscious black women's media on the continent, it is unlikely that women who have made successful journeys to their personal freedom will feel comfortable speaking about their paths to emancipation from the ties of patriarchy. As a result, their stories are lost and young women have alarmingly few role models to point the way. Essentially, as a result, African female feminists are trapped in a cycle of always being the first.

This denial of voice has implications for the extent to which women can use the power of their imagination. Imagination is the necessary link between desiring and doing. Imagination collapses the distance between the obtaining conditions and what is desired. Imagination represents the desired as a potential reality, and maps pathways of action for attaining that reality. The realised products of imagination disseminate ideas into groups, which engage the individual at the level of thought, philosophy and ideology. Tapping into a black feminist imaginary deposits black feminist representations of the world into societies and communities, enabling these black feminist representations of the world to influence other people's thinking and imagining in the direction of a world conceived by a black feminist mind. In the same way that it is necessary for black conservative patriarchal societies, and in particular African ones, to keep feminists unable to control the production of commodities and thus render us unable to gather material value to ourselves, it is also imperative for the same conservative patriarchal society to ensure that feminists are prevented from incubating feminist ideas. The capacity of ideas to inspire others derives from this: it is in the nature of ideas – a word derived from the ancient Greek *idein*, to see – to infuse energy and life into the intellect, hearts, minds and souls of others, in other words to cause internal sight. Thus feminist ideas are suppressed.

It is precisely because of this that the imaginative work of black feminists is frustrated. While white feminists imagine a world patterned along the lines of white private ownership patriarchy, in which rewards are merely redistributed, black feminists imagine a new world that has not been seen before.

We imagine a world in which, in the words of Reni Eddo-Lodge, 'all people who have been economically, socially and culturally marginalised by an ideological system that has been designed for them to fail' are liberated from the destructive effects of divisive, ranking ideologies. Eddo-Lodge points out that this means 'disabled people, black people, trans people, women and nonbinary people, LGB people and working-class people'. Black feminism envisages evened-out playing fields. It pulls down categories based on every demographic. This is big work. Referring to intersectionality, Eddo-Lodge observes, 'The idea of campaigning for equality must be complicated if we are to untangle the situation that we are in' (p. 181). This is the work at which black feminists must excel, for in their complex variety, black feminists have experienced the more repressive edge of most demographic categories and not succumbed. Black feminists are empowered by their very survival in a world constructed to relegate them to the quasi-humanity not only of race but also that of gender, and have emerged as human as any other category, if not more so. Black feminists are the demographic to imagine and energise a movement for a new, more equal society. It is for this very reason that the creative lives of black feminists are not recognised and instead extinguished. In our private moments, we African feminists laugh at the rejections we face. In the world of publishing, one of our most common jokes when comforting another sister after yet another turn-down is, 'I know, I know. They said, we've already got one of those,' meaning a black woman writer is already listed in the catalogue. And we guffaw.

People who are not black women seldom laugh at this joke. White people do not laugh because they know they are not black women and so are unable to laugh as survivors do at the thing that was meant to kill their souls and spirits, if not their bodies. Whiteness is effective because its workings are hidden. If we were fish, whiteness would have been the sea we swum in, and God help any fish that suggested the water was poisoned. White people do not know what makes them white because the world is created through white normative power: nothing pushes back at whiteness to remind it where its boundaries lie and how stifling these boundaries are. White people, of course, know very well that their normative power is directed at maiming and killing the souls of black people but they cannot admit this through laughter at a joke that points precisely at that atrocity. The laughter of white people would illuminate their whiteness. They respond by calling loud-laughing black women raucous, or look timidly on, fearing not the laughing women, but what the women are laughing at: the fact of their whiteness and all it entails; or else their eyes glaze over. Black men do not laugh either. However the reasons for black men's reasons for sternness are different from white people's. There is no guilt in it. Masculinity denies black men the harmless respite from their rejection at the hands of whiteness that black women achieve through their laughter. Black men's rage at not being taken seriously, as is said to be the due of male human beings, erupts against black – and occasionally against vulnerable white – women.

Several decades ago, while I was a film student in Berlin, I tried to articulate this to my Spanish tutor. 'How can I get that onto the screen?' I asked. 'The fact that when they look at you they do not see you?' My tutor, an amiable white Cuban male, gave me a perplexed look. I realise now he might not have known what I was talking about. The opposite – erasing something that is there is easy. Showing that something that has been said not to exist for hundreds of years – that is, the worthiness, dignity, and humanity of black people – does in fact exist is a task of Herculean proportions. It requires the utmost stamina and patience. Ensuring this recognition and pushing back against all that militates against these recognitions is the work of black feminists at its highest level. Yet, like African society, and individual white people, global society is structured to ignore the creative work of black African feminists. Its collective mind retreats, instead of engaging, even though stimulating and tapping into the imagination of feminists is critical for enabling feminist, humanist, all-emancipating contributions to society to come to fruition.

Women's, and more particularly, feminists' partic-ipation in symbolic life – those areas that rely on the imaginary for their power, such as religion, politics and the humanities, including, more latterly the creative economies, as well as women's access to public spaces where their imaginations might not be easily policed – has been vigorously controlled or prohibited in patriarchal societies. The exclusion of women and feminists from the imaginary is not limited to black women. It was only in 2021 that a woman-directed feminist film won the Palme d'Or at Cannes with Julia Ducournau's *Titane* (French for titanium), and she is white. The only other woman to win the prize before Ducournau was Jane Campion for her 1993 film *The Piano*. She was awarded the prize in a tie with Chen Kaige for his *Farewell My Concubine*. In literature, the queasiness about black women's imagination was displayed when Bernardine Evaristo was awarded the 2019 Booker Prize jointly with Margaret Atwood. I've documented my own struggles to be published both in Zimbabwe and abroad elsewhere in this volume.

As a result of the hurdles, that appear impossible to jump for many and which are intentionally constructed to appear so, many African women who have a strong sense of justice and a well-developed sense of self opt for activism rather than feminism. Activism allows black continental women to direct their phenomenal energies toward social reform through channels that are supported by one or more of the power bases operating in their societies. There are many black female activists, but few black female feminist activists. Black female feminists tend to be career feminists, rather than feminists of conscience. They utter phrases such as, 'My institution supports X, but I personally don't,' where X is some locally controversial issue such as homosexuality. I have come to understand that they exhibit externally derived agency, as opposed to internally derived agency.

External agency is an ability to act that is conferred by external factors. It provides an opportunity to act. In circumstances where opportunities to act are rare, as, for example, in black communities, such opportunities are grasped at. Escaping the drudgery of village life, a woman will tie on a ruling party print wrap, board a bus at her local stop and be driven to town for free, to enjoy the spectacle of military parades and government-supporting musical acts she would otherwise never experience. She will receive a pack of chicken and chips and a Coca-Cola for lunch. It's the Zimbabwean equivalent of *panem et circenses*. She will put her name down on any list, including a voting list when the chief in her Shepstone-inspired reserve asks her to. Come election time she will receive a few kilogrammes of rice, a delicacy not often available in the rural areas. Her family will relish the meal, and to her that's agency. She'll swagger through town on the next party trip and order cars and civilians who are not on their way to the state event at the stadium to hurry out of her way. External agency produces the mirror image of the agency-providing entity.

Internal agency is the result of battles with conscience and difficult choices where an inner morality triumphs. It is the agency that fuels choices to be visible in public as an individual, rather than to hide one's identity amidst masses. This is the sort of agency that black feminists, and in particular black African feminists of conscience, exhibit. It is the result of an unrelenting fight for survival and dignity. It transcends the self. Our conviction is deep, bolstered by a vivid imagination that reminds us that other realities are possible beyond the one that obtains. We build our theory as we go, constructing it out of our own experience. In this way we follow Toni Morrison's example of putting her black female self at the centre and never moving. It is this conscious positioning of ourselves with no respect to the arena that has been prepared for us – the fact that we have carved out a place for ourselves just as we are, in a world that would much rather we did not exist – that makes us the status quo's worst nightmare. This is why people perceive us as superwomen.

Decolonisation as
Revolutionary Imagining

Colonialism brings pain to all concerned. Some varieties of its pathology are more easily identified than others. Virginia Woolf commented how, on a bus ride in London, she saw a black man and thought to herself how terrible it was to bear the mark of humiliation.[1] I found the comment insightful and terrifying when I read it many years ago as a young woman.

Defining the pain that flows from the system of colonisation into the black body is the norm. Corporeal varieties of colonial violence that displace bodies, set boundaries on bodies, change what bodies ingest, or what kind of work bodies may do, along with the kind of products bodies may work to produce, are the subject of much attention today. We are assailed daily with immigration narratives, vaccination – or lack of vaccination – accounts, starvation stories, torture tales, police brutality chronicles and disease histories. All too seldom, in the history of the institution of Western colonisation, has discourse engaged with what may be called the metaphysical, that is the cognitive and affective – the subjective – forms of colonial violence. This is hardly surprising as colonisation was constructed purposefully to ensure that its effects were neither perceived nor questioned, and therefore not dismantled. Here, in my thinking, Marxian terms are reversed. According to Marx, relations of power between classes result from the classes' relative ownership positions with respect to infrastructure – that is, the means of production. Ownership is said to give rise to a suprastructure that is specifically constructed to defend class hierarchies anchored in differential ownership of infrastructure. In the case of colonial enterprise, a specific suprastructure, which had been created to defend certain infrastructural interests, was exported into socio-economic systems where neither the infrastructure, nor the modes of production of the colonising entity, nor the resultant suprastructure existed previously. In the colonised territory, the subjective edifice of the colonial project thus became in itself a means of production – which is to say an infrastructural element – where the product was the colonial subject. Colonial suprastructural systems formed a kind of symbolic colonial infrastructure that produced specific material relations of production and therefore of power. These relations persist to this day.

On the one hand, the global system that colonisation has constructed was consciously fashioned to camouflage its tracks through attacks not on the bodies but also on the symbolic worlds, such as religion, language and legal systems, of the people it subjugated. On the other, because of the colonial system's strategy of indirect rule, many melanated people remained unaware that practically, in global society, blackness is the low end on a scale whose opposite pole is whiteness. The writer Ama Ata Aidoo has recounted her experience of not knowing she was black until she left her native Ghana to live in Germany. It was then, by juxtaposition to whiteness in a way that excluded her, that she realised she was 'black'. Thus, while all black people live in great part in pain that is induced and maintained by the systems of colonisation, not all black people live in this pain as black-embodied beings. They live the experience of a human being in pain, as opposed to that of a specifically black human being in torment.

As a result, they can neither focus on nor direct their energies – limited as these energies are due to suffering – towards the distant cause of their trauma.

Some black people make a decision, consciously or otherwise, to reject the category 'black'. The idea of having one's humanity confined and devalued by such a qualifier is too excruciating to accept. In Zimbabwe, the question of removing Cecil Rhodes' remains from his grave at the Matobo Hills near Bulawayo has recently resurfaced. Significant numbers of people opine that such a move would only be acceptable if the remains of Mzilikazi, the Ndebele king who settled in the southern and western parts of the country in the 1860s, were also repatriated to South Africa. Differentiating between imperialist racialised extraction – in which material value was exported from its local source to the colonial metropolis in an unequal exchange justified by fictional racial attributes – and regional ethnic contestation provokes the anxiety of being labelled racist. This is so even though examples of systematic and casual racism surround and impact upon these black people in their daily lives. On the one side, they seek to dissociate themselves from the torment caused by racist constructions of the world, in order not to necessitate engaging in wrenching questions about their own human worth. On the other, they endeavour to bolster a sense of their human value by adopting a position of non-racialism that denies the existence and effects of racist systems sometimes in historical but particularly in contemporary society.

Questions of human worth revolve around one's positionality in society. In a world that produced the apartheid states of South Africa and many gradations of the same ideology, such as those practised in Southern Rhodesia, and other British colonies, the position of the colonial subject is defined in terms of degrees of distance from whiteness. The black-embodied person is always faced with the spectre of, and lives the experience daily in a myriad ways of being not-white.

In my childhood, I felt this positionality and its pain as an absence. A foster child raised in a white home, I always had the sense of there being something just over there, where I was not, that I dared not fall into, but whose existence meant that I could not fully exist where I was. I had the sensation of living beside myself, not that of integration into myself. The trauma caused by failure to integrate was so intense and so all-consuming that I could not identify with it, resulting in further distancing from myself so that identification with myself became impossible. I felt like a shadow that did not really exist. There was a general numbness in, and a grey matte dullness over all my perceptions. I never thought of myself as a being in the middle of things. I only thought of life and things existing around me. I was like the empty space at the centre of a wheel.

In this foster family where my brother and I, and later my little sister, lived, the grandmother took care of the family, and the grandfather was a wounded Second World War veteran confined to an armchair. Their son, who I'll call Daddy Henry,[2] drove an ambulance. His wife, Mummy Eve,* worked at the butcher's. They were kind people who believed in a full family life. That belief included joyful children. They took us out often, with Daddy Henry driving the family car. But joy eluded me as I could feel negative states more readily than I could positive ones. Positive states had to be intense, such as rolling down the hills of Dover, which I did often with my brother, or being told that my brother and I were taking the train to London to visit our parents, for me to

---

* Not her real name.

experience any real sense of their happening. Other people were things that existed around me, as well. They were things amongst which I, a non-person, almost a non-thing, meandered. While I knew that some of these people around me had some connection to me, I could not feel that connection. Because I could not conceive of myself as a person, I could not conceive of what a person was. After several years in England, my biological family returned to Zimbabwe, then called Rhodesia. There, my experience of being othered from everything, including myself, in the heart of colonising empire turned into the experience of being othered at its fringes.

In England my brother and I went out onto the street to play with other children. The white children rarely came to our house and I do not remember seeing another black child. In Zimbabwe, the children called my brother, sister and me *Varungu* and wouldn't play with us at an impressionable period of my childhood.

'These people don't want to play with us,' I said to my father.

'Don't call them "these people",' my father said. 'They are just the same as you are.'

My father said the words 'they are just the same

as you are' to me often. I learnt egalitarianism early. Grappling, albeit in a childish way, with the differences that separated the children around me from myself, I could not hide from the notion of blackness. I was in a decolonial frame of mind by the time I entered high school.

The first colonial Rhodesian Education Ordinance of 1899 provided for separate and unequal amenities for black and white children. After responsible government was granted to the settler colony in 1923, Southern Rhodesian educational policy prioritised fostering the kind of creative and intellectual skills that would be useful in establishing a thriving imperial territory. The commissioners came to see the country as 'a small but growing community of good European stock, planted on subtropical uplands in an extensive territory of great potential wealth. It is settled, and a native population of about twenty times its own numbers, composed of a people who are for the most part docile enough and intelligent enough to afford a large supply of labour.'[3] The education system was segregated, with the first academic school for Africans being founded in 1939 by the Church of England at St Augustine's Mission in the Eastern Highlands. This was followed by the first government school in 1946 at Goromonzi, where, incidentally, both my father and mother became students: he was head-boy in his senior year, and although no head-girl was appointed until after she had left, a boarding house has been named after my mother. A second government African secondary school was established at Fletcher, near Bulawayo, in 1954. Desegregation in the school system was slow. The process began at tertiary education, with the opening of the University of Zimbabwe in 1957, on the grounds that segregation was contrary to the philosophy of university, an argument propagated by a group of philanthropic white Rhodesians. In 1963 a coalition of independent white schools, churches and business interests came together to establish a number of bursaries for black children. However, land tenure legislation restricted the number of black children who could be enrolled at these schools to 6 per cent. Legislation also made it impossible for these schools to compete in sporting events at government schools when black children were team members. When I enrolled at one of these schools, the allocation for black students was around 3 per cent. The school itself was not prepared for what my presence would evince, and neither was I.

I had separation anxiety to begin with, due to my experience with being fostered, while my egalitarian sense made it difficult to negotiate the racialised environment in any of the docile ways that had come to be expected of Africans. I wasn't good at smiling, nor was I gregarious, preferring to spend my time on my own, reading. The contradictions I encountered and reacted to led to my being, for a considerable while, one of the less-liked Africans at the school, especially in comparison to African girls with happier faces. I was labelled a troublesome, unhappy child and came close to being expelled. One of my particularly ignominious exploits, or glorious deeds, depending on how one looks at it, occurred after the guerrilla war had intensified in the early 1970s. During the holidays, my parents, who were dedicated to the struggle, gave me a crash course in Zimbabwe's nationalist history. Back at my predominantly white school, where most of the white girls were farmers' daughters, I raised my voice – for the first and last time – during petitions at mass, to pray for the souls of Takawira and Parirenyatwa. The two men were nationalists who had been detained by Ian Smith's regime in the 1960s, and who both died in the nationalist struggle.

Tichafa Samuel Parirenyatwa, born in 1927, was Zimbabwe's first black trained physician. His grandfather was Chief Chingaira, who was executed by Rhodesian settlers. His mother was from the Tangwena people, who resisted the Rhodesian settler regime's attempts to evict them from their ancestral land in the Eastern Highlands, until a court ruling in their favour was ignored and the Rhodesian authorities descended with bulldozers to flatten the people's dwellings. In addition to being the country's first black medical doctor, Parirenyatwa was also the first vice-president of the Zimbabwe African People's Union (ZAPU). ZAPU was founded in 1961 by Joshua Nkomo. It was the third nationalist political party that Nkomo, today often called Father Zimbabwe, founded. The first of the series of nationalist political parties that Nkomo founded was the Southern Rhodesia African National Congress. This was also the first nationalist African political party in the country. Founded in 1957, it was a non-ethnic party whose nationwide platforms embraced universal suffrage, black welfare, eradication of racism in society, including in education, and free movement of all people in the country. The SRANC party was banned after just two years when the Southern

Rhodesian Prime Minister Edgar Whitehead declared a state of emergency, not only in Southern Rhodesia, but throughout the Central African Federation, consisting of Southern and Northern Rhodesia and Nyasaland, on the grounds that the party had incited violence. Following the ban, the party regrouped as the National Democratic Party (NDP) in 1960, with Nkomo as its president. When the NDP was banned in the following year, Joshua Nkomo, together with the NDP leadership, founded ZAPU, a party that exists and contests elections to this day.

Parirenyatwa served as a government medical doctor at a time when racial tensions were egregious. On one occasion, while Parirenyatwa was engaged in performing an autopsy, a white man burst in and tried to stop him, saying: 'No black bastard is going to cut up my mother.'[4] Following several postings, he resigned from government service in 1961 when he opened private surgeries that allowed him to engage in political work while continuing his medical career. An outstanding organiser, he was killed the following year while on the way to a political meeting in an incident Rhodesian authorities recorded as a railway accident, but Zimbabwean nationalist accounts call assassination.

Leopold Takawira joined the NDP at its founding and continued his political work with ZAPU after the NDP was banned. With time, however, many politicians became disillusioned with ZAPU's pacifist struggle. In 1963, Takawira left ZAPU to join a breakaway party, the Zimbabwe African National Union (ZANU) led by Ndabaningi Sithole. The following year, the Southern Rhodesian government detained Takawira at Sikombela Camp, near Gokwe, a small town in central Zimbabwe. A diabetic, Takawira was moved to Salisbury Prison where he died in 1970, due to inadequate medical care.

My mother told me some of this history. On the day I made my petition, everyone at the mass from my 95 per cent white school prayed for the nationalists' souls.

There were three detention centres to which African nationalists were sent by the white minority government. The Rhodesian authorities used both imprisonment and detention as a means of supressing Zimbabwean nationalist political organisation. Imprisonment was governed by the penal code. Sentences were finite and the imprisoned could regain their freedom when the period of imprisonment came to an end. Detention on the other hand was a less regulated system of freedom deprivation. It was a carefully brutal institution, intended to render the detainees dead to society to contain their influence. Detainees were not charged with any offence, nor were they accorded the right to be presumed innocent until proven guilty, or to stand trial; some had been tried in court and found not guilty. The white settler government simply picked up people it designated as politically dangerous and dumped them in detention camps for indefinite periods, often after having subjected the detainees to torture. Terms were not regulated by law. An expired detention period could simply be renewed by the Rhodesian authorities. Detention camps were located in remote areas, most of them miles from human habitation. Shelters – either barracks or rondavels that as time went on grew overcrowded – were built of corrugated iron so that they were intensely hot during the day and severely cold during the night and in winter. The quality of provisions declined steadily with time, until detainees were fed little else but stiff porridge made of maize meal, called *sadza*. The extremely remote, inaccessible locations of the camps, together with the fact that they were situated in areas densely populated with large wild animals such as lions, elephants and buffalo, were deterrents both to detainees escaping and to visitors. Being wounded by an animal was a sentence to slow, painful death, or one ran the risk of being reported and recaptured if one sought assistance. The detainees had no way of knowing whether or not there were informers in the surrounding villages who would report escapees to the authorities. Finally there was nowhere to go. Returning to family or colleagues was to put anyone who could assist in grave danger. The chances of recapture were high, in which event the sentence would be yet harsher, possibly a death penalty. As a result, the authorities believed there was no need to supervise the camps, apart from infrequent visits when they delivered provisions.

The camps' wider objective was to render the detainees dead not only to society and political struggle, but also to strip away their perception of themselves as freedom fighters. Quite to the contrary, the camps themselves became important sites of mental decolonisation. The detainees actively created societies that provided a new social formation that enabled them to cultivate their identity as freedom fighters. Fostering a spirit of defiance through academic and political education, the detained men smuggled written critiques of colonialism from the camps into the wider society where the documents fired the imagination of ordinary citizens. At the same time, they reinvented the detention camps as locations of initiation into a more heroic level of struggle. New recruits were greeted with whistling, applause and congratulations at being elevated to a more potent and effective masculinity in service of freedom from colonial rule. Detainees recommitted to the struggle and expanded their mental, intellectual and emotional capacity to prosecute it. Before Ian Smith made a Unilateral Declaration of Independence in 1965, there were no supervisors or guards at the camps, nor were boundaries marked by fences, so that once they had settled in, detainees travelled considerable distances on foot to engage with local peasant communities in order to politicise them against the Rhodesian authorities.

———

Once the nationalists had wrested independence from the Rhodesian settlers, black Zimbabweans were ready to see its systems dismantled at every level, ranging from the offices and policies of state to petty manifestations in the streets and classrooms.

In spite of the nationalists' victory at the political level, however, the decolonisation project did not remain on the ZANU PF political agenda for long after the 1980 independence celebrations. By means of a ferociously partisan military-political elite, ZANU PF adopted strategies designed to reproduce colonial hegemonies in its systems and practices of rulership. Just as in settler times, violence was and continues to this day to be a staple part of the ZANU PF government's strategy. The 1983–7 genocide in Matabeleland, in which it is estimated twenty thousand people were murdered, is well documented. Violence escalated again in 2000 following the formation of the Movement for Democratic Change (MDC) and the contestations, including conflicts around land, which took place at the time the new party was formed. The presidential elections of 2002 contested by incumbent Robert Mugabe of ZANU PF and Morgan Tsvangirai of the MDC as frontrunners, saw another escalation in violence. In 2005, Operation Murambatsvina (Operation Refusal of Dirt) preceded the parliamentary election. This violent government action destroyed the homes and/or livelihoods of seven hundred thousand urban citizens, and displaced over 2 million more, the urban centres being seen as MDC strongholds. Meanwhile Alex Magaisa tells us of unprecedented levels of state-sponsored violence between the end of March and 27 June 2008, which was associated with a presidential election in which Robert Mugabe of ZANU PF and Morgan Tsvangirai of the MDC were again frontrunners.[5] Two hundred people were killed, while five thousand more were assaulted and thirty-six thousand were displaced. Less than a decade later, the violence invaded ZANU PF itself with the events that led to the coup of November 2017. The Zimbabwe Human Rights NGO Forum informs that organised violence and torture has increased in Zimbabwe since November 2017 when the coup occurred. There were twenty-four abductions, i.e. kidnappings, said to have been effected by state agents in 2018. In the same year government forces shot at civilians with live ammunition during a demonstration to protest election results. At least six deaths and more casualties were reported. In 2019, there were sixty-seven abductions. In 2020, fifteen abductions were reported, eleven of them tied to a 31 July protest. The abductions typically are said to be accompanied by beatings and torture. Some forms of torture are alleged to be physical, while others are said to be degrading, designed to break a person down and deprive a person of dignity. During the Matabeleland genocide, even more grotesque forms of torture, designed to break down a person's actual sense of humanity, were practised.

While the indignity and inhumanity of torture arouse outrage in many sectors today, the slow erosion of self-worth that accompanies chronic poverty receives less notice. Rather, the glitter, glamour and power associated with wealth draw attention and spark desire. While the nationalists fought on a platform of wealth redistribution, Zimbabwe has remained an enclave economy under ZANU PF. As during the colonial era, wealth continues to be extracted from human resources through taxes and from natural resources through speculative, unregulated business deals in order to benefit power elites and their enablers.

In addition to economic exploitation and systematic degradation, historical records confirm direct, systematic and savage settler viciousness practised on citizens. Officials of the British South Africa Charter Company (BSACC), the private company founded by Cecil Rhodes in 1889, used brutal tactics to bring the local people to heel when their authority was disregarded. In 1892 the royal house of Moghabi in north-eastern Zimbabwe refused to recognise the private company's jurisdiction in a dispute with another royal house. The company's police force, the British South Africa Police (BSAP), executed the Moghabi royal personage. In the same month, February, a European person was killed in the same territory. As the murderer was not identified, the BSACC held a particular royal house responsible. They burnt several homesteads belonging to the royal house and captured its royal personage. Complaints of theft by white people led to the homestead of the local leader being led to the local leader's homestead being burnt and numbers of people under the leaders' jurisdiction being executed.[6] The early settlers in Zimbabwe and many other parts of the British empire ruled by terror. The writer Ngũgĩ wa Thiong'o conjures up the brutality of this modus operandi in his observation that it is impossible to picture the settler without a rawhide whip called a sjambok in hand. The name 'sjambok' for such a whip is ubiquitous in British southern and eastern African former colonies. It entered the English language in the nineteenth century from the Afrikaans, which had it from the Malay word *samboq*.

The word travelled to South Africa with Malay slaves enslaved by Dutch slave traders, who themselves had the word from Urdu. Royal charter companies such as the British South Africa Charter Company operated throughout the European empires. Following its founding by the BSACC, the Rhodesian state became progressively more repressive. Its legislation disadvantaged the African population in every sector of life, ranging from where people could live or be at particular times given pass laws, what economic opportunities they could benefit from, which social goods they could access and imposition of extractive tax laws that forced men into labour at little more than slave wages. It was a system of racialised serfdom.

These colonial practices affected the black population at both physical and psychological levels. Consider the hypothetical case of a hungry child, whose parents have been moved from a more fertile area where they had previously grown enough produce to feed the family, and who were subsequently confined to a reservation, that omnipresent colonial institution of land expropriation located in barren areas. The parents are no longer able to grow enough food to feed their child.

After much hunger, that the child hopes will come

to an end, but which does not, the child asks finally, 'Mother, why do you not feed me?'

The mother answers, 'I do not feed you because the white person prevents me from doing so.'

The mother practises single parenting because the male parent has gone to work in the towns or mines. After a long period of waiting for the father to return, the child asks, 'Mother, why is Father not here?'

The mother answers, 'He cannot come back because he has gone to work for the white people who do not give him enough money to be able to come back to see us, since what he earns goes to pay the white people the hut tax they have imposed on these buildings we built to live in.'

The chronic psychological distress caused by living under such barbarity needed to be managed. Africans adjusted to this ceaseless experience of want by defining themselves as not possessing that which a person required to lead a dignified life. The armed struggle that followed the failure of the political struggle for majority rule mentioned above, whose first battle took place in 1966, did not rectify this situation. To the dismay of Zimbabweans already damaged by decades of colonial oppression, the war resulted in further psychological trauma. It is generally accepted that nationalist guerrillas killed more black civilians than they killed Rhodesian security forces or white Rhodesians. It is said that one reason for the guerrillas' use of extreme violence against black Zimbabweans was to punish traitors and anyone who collaborated with the Rhodesian regime. Another reason was to overcome the disincentive of Rhodesian retribution, because Rhodesian vengeance strongly inhibited practical expression of the political support with which the black population in general favoured the guerrillas. Guerrilla violence was thus a tactic to overcome fear of Rhodesian reprisal and the attraction of rewards the Rhodesian regime offered, through instilling into the majority population a fear of consequences of non-cooperation with the nationalist effort, which was greater than the fear that the black majority experienced for the Rhodesian regime and its army. Thus, at the hands of the guerrillas also, the people experienced profound trauma, both physical and psychological.

There has been little psychological rehabilitation from this long history of trauma. ZANU PF post-independence brutality and evil misgovernance has simply worsened the torment. The repressive colonial hierarchy remains, with a different demographic occupying the positions of power. Thus, it is still common, in Zimbabwe, to hear a person, who perceives themself as being of lower status than another, to address that other, of perceived higher status, as *murungu wangu* – 'my white person'. Equating *murungu* to higher status than 'me' points to the way in which colonisation was practised through restructuring the content of the mind as well as through occupying the land of the colonised and coercing their bodies. Just as physical bodies were moved from the land in order to allow white settlers to appropriate the land, it was also necessary to remove mental contents from minds and to replace them with other contents, to ensure that the moved bodies acquiesced to their moving and their repurposing not to be subjects in their own right, but objects in service of the colonial project.

African identity had, in any case, never conformed to European conceptualisations of identity. Kinship structures that conferred rather rigid, hierarchical roles on individuals in an extended family network left little room for negotiating ego drives outside of the network of relationship. At the same time, these roles conferred different identities according to the identity of the one with whom an individual negoti-ated a relationship, that is to say, encountered at any given moment. A person was, for example, at the same time a youngest son, a brother, an uncle, a nephew, niece, son, daughter and grandchild, with distinct ways of behaviour in each of these roles. Any number of these roles might be enacted within the course of a day or an hour. Moreover, they changed with age, and, because marriage introduced a person into a new kinship network where their role was different, with marriage. Behaviour considered appropriate differed across these different relationships and that was socially acceptable. It did not in any way signal fickleness or lack of character, rather knowing how to behave well in every situation one found oneself in. Identity has therefore always been more fluid in such settings, with a person occupying many roles and therefore bearing many identities simultaneously. Accordingly, it was well within the realm of possibil-ity to conceive of oneself as both contained within a framework of whiteness that conferred inferiority, and as a fully realised individual in one's own community circles. Everyone was functioning within the context of whiteness and made similar identity adjustments. In this way, identity modulation by the colonial subject produced behaviours that enabled physical survival without enduring extreme sanction from the colonial systems. The identity of realised individual within one's own community enabled recreation and a degree of reintegration. Apartheid divisions in the social structure enabled this dissociation. Thus developed the phenomenon of double consciousness, which is an enduring aspect of the colonial subject's subjectivity, together with the hypervigilance that has the colonial subject ever on the alert to the coloniser's whims and strategies of whim fulfilment.

The ability to dissociate with some degree of immediate success flows from a pragmatic approach to life that values survival at any cost. The African philosophy of *ubuntu*, founded on the now well-known premise 'I am well if you are too', is grounded in such pragmatism. The phrase is a greeting prevalent in my language group in Zimbabwe, whose underlying meaning can be rendered thus: If we all get on well together and each of us makes sure the other is well, we will all be well. The *nhimbe* is one example of a behavioural expression of this philosophy. A *nhimbe* was essentially a work party, in which the families in a community grouped together to work each family's fields. Another expression of the *ubuntu* philosophy is the practice of *zunde ramambo*, the 'shelter' of the king. This was a kind of welfare tax in which families gave a certain portion of their yield to the royal personage who presided over its distribution to vulnerable families. Then the 'exploration' of Africa began, coinciding with the destitution of the English state under the Tudors in the late sixteenth and early seventeenth centuries. The British Crown established and deployed royal charter companies throughout the British empire, with the devastating result that three-quarters of the world is still to recover from the system.

That India was the fourth richest polity in the world prior to British colonisation is now also well known. Africa, in particular Southern Africa, was introduced into the British empire relatively late as imperial commercial routes stretched from western ports, including English ones to Asia, and the Americas. Kehinde Andrews relates how the often cruel and deadly competition and conflict of European state formation from the sixteenth century onwards always turned into a kind of a north-western European '*nhimbe*' of control when it came to maintaining the colonies in a state of subjugation.[7] European states may have competed for resources, including colonial resources, amongst themselves, but they united in their desire to either erase from the face of the earth people on whose land they settled, or to subjugate them completely. It was a grotesque kind of work party, resulting in some of the worst atrocities in history, including the genocide of brown-skinned people in the Americas and Pacific, and black-skinned people on the African continent.

White supremacy was invented during the Enlightenment, premised on theories of black sub-humanity. Thought and knowledge patterns of the modern West began to take shape during the Enlightenment. This period of European transformation was fortified by genocide and pillage in the Americas and Caribbean that ushered in the transatlantic slave trade. A hundred years after Christopher Columbus landed on the shores of an island known to the local inhabitants as Guanahani, in the group of islands today called the Bahamas, an intellectual rationale for the pillage that followed was a psychological necessity. Racial theories invented by European philosophers during the Enlightenment provided an intellectual justification for categoris-ation of people according to physiological markers that to this day include skin colour, hair texture, body proportions and shape of facial features, amongst others. The nature of membership of these categories was, and continues to be, used to rank people on the scale of animal to human, with highly melanated people occupying the animal end, and lesser melanated people occupying the human end of the scale. European traders in enslaved people routinely referred to the dark-skinned people of Africa whom they enslaved as 'human cattle'. Immanuel Kant, who wrote in the second half of the eighteenth century, stated 'humanity is at its greatest perfection in the race of the whites. The yellow Indians do have a meagre talent. The Negroes are far below them.'[8] Referring to black Africans, Kant opined, 'they can be educated but only as servants, that is they allow themselves to be trained'. His advice was to discipline a Negro by use of 'a cane but it has to be a split one, so that the cane will cause wounds large enough that prevent suppuration underneath the "Negro's" thick skin'. Voltaire in France wrote, 'None but the blind can doubt that the Whites, the Negroes, the Albinoes [sic], the Hottentots, the Laplanders, the Chinese, the Americans, are races entirely different.' The idea that Africans behave like eternal children as 'they are sold and let themselves be sold without any reflection on the rights or wrongs of the matter' was propagated by Hegel in Germany. Aligning with continental European thought Englishman John Locke believed that 'Negroes' were the product of African women sleeping with apes and therefore that we were subhuman. Meanwhile in Scotland, David Hume more or less paraphrased Kant concerning the superiority of white men over other human beings, as did Thomas Jefferson across the Atlantic. Knowledge that is founded on notions of inequality will build unequal worlds for humans to occupy and unequal systems for us to function in.

Western civilisation has been bloody as far back as, and even before, the first century of the Christian Era when the Romans invaded Britain and found the British so primitive and backward as scarcely to be worthwhile as slaves. Genocide, slavery and colonisation are the DNA not just of the modern Western empire, but of all empire. In this way the specific path of exploitation of the world practised by Western empire can be seen as a continuation of the practices of subjugation they suffered under the Roman empire of the Mediterranean basin, through appropriation of its legacy. There was no rupture in the logic of empire from classical times in

European thought and practice. The Roman empire continued to serve as a symbol of power and prestige until modern times. It is difficult to imagine a Western logic that is not built on empire and its gory precedents.

Although white men are today's go-to villains, white men were not the only white gender that prosecuted the practice of colonisation. Andrews informs us:

> While we remember the brave male pioneers of genocide, slavery and colonialism, it was Queen Isabella of Spain who gave the green light to this new world 'discovery' and Queen Elizabeth I who launched Britain's industrial involvement in the slave trade when she assented to John Hawkins' mission on the slave ship *Jesus*.

It is this progression of history, shaped by white men and women over half a millennium, that has laid the foundation for the ongoing brutality of racialised inequality in today's socio-economic relations. This inequality was exported from Britain and other European states where society was highly stratified. Thus the work of decolonisation, while most obviously urgent in the post-colonies, needs to stretch back to embrace the drivers of colonisation that lay and continue to work in the social and economic structures of Great Britain and Europe's other colonising nations.

Historical relationships between more melanated and lesser melanated people have given rise to phobic relations between the categories. Fanon, writing about the French occupation of Algeria, has pointed out how the 'Negro' (Fanon's term) is a phobogenic object, a stimulus to anxiety.[9] This phobogenesis is effective in two directions, with the result that lesser melanated people are affected in dual ways. On the one hand there was and continues to be the terror that the more melanated people might one day rise up to exact vengeance in unspeakable ways, the so-called 'black peril'. On the other, lesser melanated people experience guilt about their forebears' behaviour, and thus fear of that which reminds them of this guilt. The body of the melanated person comes to personify this guilt. The fear experienced by lesser melanated people drives their investment in continuing structures of economic and social enterprise that subjugate people of Africa. For them this fear is one aspect of the existential fear that we all experience as time-bound humans whose period of earthly existence stretches between the transitions of birth and death.

The melanated person, in contrast, has lived in a world structured according to the ego-world of lesser melanated people, a world spoken and acted into being by the collective 'I' of white society. Since melanated people were excluded from it, this world constantly declared 'not being as I am, you are a not-I' to black people. The world we live in structures our affective, behavioural and perceptive worlds. Thus the melanated people who live in the world of white people – which all of us to a greater or lesser extent do – come to identify with themselves as 'not-I', also to a greater or lesser extent, or must expend significant time, energy and resources in building up and retaining a healthy sense of their own unnegated, that is positive, being. At the negated end of the scale, their very bodies become an object of terror to themselves. Fear management in melanated people also manifests in a variety of ways. Individuals may become apathetic and depressed. Others may become enraged. Both are reactions to the interruption of their being, historically in the displacement and other traumas experienced by their forebears, and today due to the interruption of their hopes and aspirations through the imposition of the category of blackness. The depressed become the unproductive melanated people who conform to the stereotype of docility and incompetence. The enraged become the disruptive melanated people who must be managed. These are two ends of the spectrum, with many gradations between them. No melanated person's capacity to function has escaped being affected in some disruptive way by the white-centred structures of the world they live in. Other melanated people became complicit. To these black people, colonialism was benign. They go out of their way to cooperate with and uphold its structures. Complicity may be conscious or unconscious, and such complicit melanated people are often rewarded for their acquiescence to the demands of a white world with economic elevation, or with other rewards that are valued in that world, such as social stature.

Complicity was often the most rational choice, one that guaranteed staying alive. Amidst the guns and sjamboks, the missionaries with their services, communion and Bibles, and the settlers' encroachment, it was pragmatic to take what was on offer to extend or improve life, a life that was wretched for those who did not submit. If the education, job or military uniform that enabled one to live in relative peace came at the price of making the body useful to the colonial enterprise, so be it. This is how my parents came to take up scholarships to study for their master's degrees at University College London. This is how I came not to be for many years, and how my coming into being, past and present, requires filling in a great chasm, which I constantly seek to do with words. The guns were silent by then, but the fundamental structure of relationships persisted, as they do into the present.

By the time my parents arrived in England in 1961, for the British leg of their education, Africans had been arriving in the United Kingdom for tertiary education for decades. Many arrived under the watchful eye of the Colonial Office. At first students – who at that time were all male – relocated from their homes to the United Kingdom alone, leaving their wives or children behind. The colonial authorities observed that on returning home, these students found it difficult to reintegrate with their families. They were also concerned about significant numbers of relationships and marriages between the African students and British women that resulted from single black men being present in the United Kingdom. In 1955 the

Colonial Office altered its policy to encourage the male students to travel with their families. The very same year the first advertisement seeking foster care for African children in Britain appeared in a London magazine.[10] By 1960 there were eleven thousand recognised African students – mostly Ghanaians and Nigerians – studying in the United Kingdom, many of whose children were cared for privately in foster homes. White working-class homes were the destination for the African children, who on their return to Africa were expected to be middle class. Kent, Surrey, East Sussex, Hertfordshire, and Essex were typical destinations.[11]

Little is known about the consequences of foster care at that time. When I was mature enough and calm enough to talk to her rationally about it, my mother told me she thought fostering approximated the extended family arrangements that were common and continue to be common in Zimbabwe and in other African social structures. In any case, African parents found the rigours of childcare in the English environment a challenge. The wives often studied, too. Nigerian novelist Buchi Emecheta was to write, in her novel *Second Class Citizen*, 'At home in Nigeria, all a mother had to do for a baby was wash and feed him and, if he was fidgety, strap him onto her back and carry on with her work while that baby slept. But in England she had to wash piles and piles of nappies, wheel the child round for sunshine during the day, attend to his feeds as regularly as if one were serving a master, talk to the child, even if he was only a day old! Oh, yes, in England, looking after babies was in itself a full-time job.'[12] I could understand why my mother had opted to have the two children she brought with her from Southern Rhodesia and the one she bore in england fostered, but I don't think she ever understood what the experience did to us. I hope she didn't.

Accounts of the devastating effect of fostering on African heritage children have begun to emerge. Shola Amoo's 2019 film *The Last Tree*, which premiered at the Sundance Film Festival, depicts a Nigerian boy's struggle to connect with his biological mother in London on his return to her after being fostered in Lincolnshire. Other African children fostered in the 1970s and 1980s ended up in therapy.[13] Most of the accessible accounts are of children who returned to live with their biological parent or parents in England. Returning to Africa added another dimension to the rupture. Back in

Mutare in the 1960s, my brother used to tell me, 'Tsitsi, I don't really belong to this family. I'm adopted.' I did not know the desperate call for help his words were until I was an adult, by which time it was too late. He did not make it. There is not a day when I do not think about how colonisation ripped through my family, and yet, in spite of scratching my nipples off and cutting myself with glass as a child – all of which went unnoticed in my foster home – and mourning a brother who died too young, I am one of those whose experience is mild compared to millions of others over the centuries, and who has managed to achieve some success in my life as an intellectual and a producer of narrative in various media. Yet spaces for our discursive products remain small, opportunities constrained, and our output is undervalued across all sectors.

As recently as November 2021, Boris Johnson's government reminded us how white supremacy is part of the DNA of British society. On 9 November a Botswana laboratory, run by a Zimbabwean virologist, identified and began sequencing a new variant of the Covid-19 virus, which would later be named Omicron. South Africa also sequenced the virus and relayed the information it found to the world on 25

November. The United Kingdom placed travel bans on travellers from eleven southern African countries almost immediately. Other countries followed suit. The German newspaper *Die Rheinpfalz* carried an article headlined, 'The virus from Africa is here,' while the Spanish newspaper *La Tribuna de Albacete* published a cartoon showing a load of virus variants with brown skin and coiled hair in a boat with a South African flag approaching a shore where a European Union flag stood. Both newspapers apologised for their publications following outcries from a diverse public, and that is progress. Nevertheless the fact that such publications were made at all indicates that white supremacist anti-black ideology is still a normal part of twenty-first-century relations. Instead of Botswana and South Africa being complimented for their excellent science, these African countries and their citizens were punished. The travel bans themselves reinforced in the eyes of the world that Africa is a diseased and dangerous place, even though it was known that the Covid-19 virus originated in China and the Omicron variant was present in European countries before it was sequenced in Botswana.

While we are all affected by modernity's systems that destroy human and other life, as well as the planet itself, and we all need to shed its effects if we are to prolong our presence on our planet and maximise well-being for the greatest number of people and life forms, we have different tasks. Melanated people are still wading through swamps of negativity, still grasping for the vital principle that was removed when our being was siphoned from our bodies by the forces of colonisation. Our suffering is the metaphysical equivalent of a phantom limb.

———

We are at a moment of decision-making concerning which knowledges we will use to plot our future and which logic we will permit to guide us past the challenges of our age, such as climate change, sustainability, immigration and inequality. The earth and its systems are not open. We cannot change the earth, a fact that leaves us with no choice but to change ourselves. Escaping to another planet will not help, much as we may wish it might. We will simply take destructive white supremacist ideology with us if we do not make different choices first. This moment is at least as foundational to how to move forward as the decisions taken during the Enlightenment were to the path of that era. If the logic of the Enlightenment was racism, slavery, genocide and colonisation, decolonisation is the only logic that offers hope for the future. The logic of empire still reigns. A 2014 survey shows that 59 per cent of Britons think that the empire was something to be proud of.[14] A half a millennium old practice is hard to uproot, whatever one's melanin concentration. Yet the trajectory of current and future generations depends on that uprooting.

An advertisement I saw while walking in Schöneberg, Berlin, advised, 'Fight racism on the street and in the head.' 'Street' means the public sphere, where people from diverse groupings gather and may confer to agree on and initiate action. 'Head' refers to individual cognito-affective systems. It is these individual cognito-affective systems that gather in public space to confer and initiate action. Thus our cognitive-affective systems are the only true site of decolonisation. Decolonisation that frees all from fear requires a new revolution of the imaginary and its products. This revolution of the imaginary and new imaginative production can only be affected by bringing to consciousness the discursive products of those who have been relegated to the subjective status of 'not-I', in spite of the anxiety and fear that this 'not-I' and therefore its products may induce in most of us. These discursive products of black imagination and endeavour have been suppressed and devalued by the systems of the colonial enterprise – social, political and economic – for centuries, and continue to be. Not working towards discursive equality will hold us on our present trajectory. There are signs that this trajectory will, perhaps sooner than we expected, bring us to a place of pain that exceeds the pain of confronting the colonial 'not-I', a spectre that hangs over all of us.

Notes

Introduction

1   L. I. Izuakor, 'Kenya: The Unparamount African Paramountcy', *Transafrican Journal of History* 12 (1983), pp. 33–50.
2   W. R. Whaley, 'Race Policies in Rhodesia', *Zambezia* 3:2 (1973), pp. 31–7, journals.co.za/doi/pdf/10.10520/AJA03790622_369.
3   Alan Cousins, 'State, Ideology, and Power in Rhodesia, 1958–1972', *The International Journal of African Historical Studies* 24:1 (1991), pp. 35–64.
4   Chengetai J. M. Zvobgo, 'Shona and Ndebele Responses to Christianity in Southern Rhodesia, 1897–1914', *Journal of Religion in Africa*, 8:1 (1976), pp. 41–51.

Writing While Black and Female

1   *Twelve Years a Slave*, dir. Steve McQueen, 2013.
2   I have changed this person's name for privacy reasons.
3   Kimberlé Crenshaw, *On Intersectionality: The Essential Writings of Kimberlé Crenshaw*, The New Press, New York, 2019.

Black, Female and the Superwoman Black Feminist

1 Simon Coldham 'The Status of Women in Zimbabwe: *Veneria Magaya v. Nakayi Shonhiwa Magaya* (SC 210/98)', *Journal of African Law*, 43:2 (1999), pp. 248–52.
2 Coldham, 'Status of Women'.
3 Reni Eddo-Lodge, *Why I'm No Longer Talking to White People about Race*, Bloomsbury, London, 2018, p. 4.

Decolonisation as Revolutionary Imagining

1 Entry for 17 May 1925, *The Diary of Virginia Woolf, vol. 3: 1925–1930*, ed. Anne Olivier Bell and Andrew McNeillie, Harvest/HBJ: New York and London, 1981, p. 23.
2 We called the son and daughter-in-law Daddy and Mummy, followed by their first names. I have changed the names.
3 Norman Atkinson, 'Racial Integration in Zimbabwean Schools', 1979–1980, *Comparative Education*, 8:1 (1982), pp. 77–89.
4 Luise White, 'The Traffic in Heads: Bodies, Borders and the Articulation of Regional Histories', *Journal of Southern African Studies*, 23:2, Special Issue for Terry Ranger (June 1997), pp. 325–38.
5 Alex Magaisa, 'BSR: Presidential Amnesty and Impunity in Zimbabwe', BSR [blog], 22 April 2016, bigsr.africa/the-big-saturday-read-

presidential-amnesty-a-short-history-of-
impunity-and-political-violence-in-zimbabwe-d93/.

6 John S. Galbraith, *Crown and Charter, The Early Years of the British South Africa Company*, UC Press, 2021.

7 Kehinde Andrews, *The New Age of Empire: How Racism and Colonialism Still Rule the World*, Penguin, 2021.

8 Andrews.

9 Frantz Fanon, *Black Skin, White Masks*, trans. Charles Lam Markmann, London: Pluto Press, 1986.

10 Jordanna Bailkin, 'The Postcolonial Family? West African Children, Private Fostering, and the British State', *The Journal of Modern History*, 81: 1 (March 2009), pp. 87–121.

11 Bailkin.

12 Buchi Emecheta, *Second Class Citizen*, Penguin Random House UK, 2021.

13 Ade Onibada, '5 People Shared With Us How Being "Farmed" To White Families Impacted Their Lives And How They See Race', Buzzfeed News, 10 Oct. 2019, www.buzzfeed.com/adeonibada/ farming-foster-care-black-children-white-families.

14 Will Dahlgreen, 'The British Empire is "something to be proud of"', YouGov [blog], 26 July 2014, yougov.co.uk/top-ics/politics/articles-reports/2014/07/26/ britain-proud-its-empire.

Acknowledgements

Little over a year ago, Karolina Sutton asked me whether I write non-fiction. I responded that I did. Little did I know that Karolina already had a project in mind that would become this collection of essays. I am indebted to her for asking the right question at the right time and for her advice to me to slow down, which I shall remember for the rest of my days.

My response was only a half truth. I had not, in fact, written non-fiction for publication, my attempts in that direction having been lectures and speeches. Not quite sure what I would do, once I had signed the contract, Jessica Craig came to the rescue with her commission of a non-fiction piece and her infinite patience with my horrific first draft. Much credit for the good things in these essays is due to the excellent guidance I received from Jessica, while the faults in it are entirely the result of my being a less than conscientious student.

My publisher, Louisa Joyner's keen feeling for rhythm, her sense of clarity and her sensitivity to nuance brought my initial meanderings into shape in the kindest way possible. I am grateful and always will be.

At a time when I grappled with access to the research I needed, the University of Stellenbosch offered me a Research Fellowship at the Department of English. This post allowed me to use the Stellenbosch University Library. It is not an exaggeration to say I would not have been able to write these essays without the facilities the fellowship offered. I am much obliged to the University of Stellenbosch.

Finally, I thank my husband Olaf Koschke for his love and support that has him unearthing rare texts for me at any time of the day or night and who endures with me all my writerly afflictions, yet astonishingly still has sufficient energy to celebrate with me each time a work comes to completion.